26/6/87
(Cley) juv.

THE NATURAL & UNNATURAL HISTORY OF NORFOLK'S BIRDS

THE NATURAL & UNNATURAL HISTORY OF NORFOLK'S BIRDS

(Originally published as *Bird of the Month* in the *Norfolk Journal*)

David North

Illustrated by Frank Jarvis

A limited first edition of 1,000 copies

This copy No: 936

Blue Sky Publications

To my Mother and the memory of my Father

Blue Sky Publications / David North
1 Chapel Terrace, The Street, Sculthorpe, Fakenham, Norfolk NR21 9QD

A limited first edition of 1,000 copies

ISBN 09522164 5 0

Printed by Broadgate Printers, Aylsham Norfolk NR11 6SS
Further copies of this publication may be purchased from Blue Sky Publications / David North at the above address.

Contents

Preface

Norfolk is Britain's premier birdwatching county. It can be justly proud of its range of breeding birds, which includes several exciting national rarities; Marsh Harrier, Avocet, Bearded Tit and Bittern amongst them.

Today Norfolk is a mecca for birdwatchers, but in the past sites like Blakeney Point were equally attractive to Victorian collectors who came to shoot and stuff rather than to watch and wonder. In fact one has only to visit the bird gallery at the Castle Museum in Norwich to appreciate part of the toll of Norfolk's rarities which fell to the guns of these Victorian collectors. The loss during the nineteenth century of Avocet, Ruff, Marsh Harrier and Bittern as breeding birds can hardly be described as natural history when the birds were so ruthlessly persecuted. Equally the conservation success stories of this century, prime amongst them being the return of the beautiful Avocet, have been just as much determined by the hand of man. Without the creation of many fine Norfolk nature reserves, Titchwell, Cley Marshes and Blakeney Point to name just a few, many rare birds, including the Avocet, would not have prospered.

The story of Norfolk's birds, and their changes in numbers and distribution, is also a history of man's impact on the Norfolk landscape. The huge reduction in numbers of birds such as Lapwing, and the extinction of Ruffs as a breeding bird, reflect centuries of drainage of their wetland and marshland haunts. Birds are superb indicators of environmental change, and the dangers of particular pesticides used during the 1950s and 1960s were first indicated by the massive decline in Kestrel and Sparrowhawk populations.

Man has always had an impact on the natural history of the birds which live close to him; creating new habitats, often destroying old ones. The decline of the Nightjar this century has mirrored the destruction of its heathland habitat, but the upturn in numbers in recent decades has equally been a response to the creation of new habitats in the vast conifer woodlands that now cover much of Breckland. The fortunes of both our gamebirds and birds of prey are inextricably linked to the activities of gamekeepers and the management of large Norfolk estates. Indeed, if Pheasants have a natural history then it is confined to the Himalayan regions where these birds are truly native!

This relationship between man and birds has not been one-way. Man may have affected birds, both for good and bad, but equally birds have found their way into the human psyche, as symbols of good or bad luck, or simply as sources of joy and inspiration. We may no longer think that the eerie call of the Nightjar is the voice of the souls of dead, unbaptised children, or that to see a Magpie is bad luck, but the colours and songs of the birds that surround us still bring contact with nature into even the most built-up environments. The first Swift or Swallow, and the Cuckoo's call, are powerful symbols of the changing seasons. Something within us still responds to the clarion calls of geese in autumn, freshly arrived from Arctic breeding grounds. They speak to us of wilderness and wild places. Perhaps few of us who care for Norfolk are lucky enough ever to have seen a Bittern in one of its last remaining haunts along the North Norfolk coast. Yet many who have never seen one will agree that if we do lose the Bittern from Norfolk, a little magic will die with them and Norfolk will be somehow less mysterious and poorer for their passing.

This book is dedicated to those who, whilst they may not know the name of every bird they see, can still delight in the birds, both common and rare, that are part of Norfolk's special appeal. Most of all, I hope this book will add to the readers' enjoyment when they next meet up with some of its subjects – the endlessly fascinating birds of Norfolk.

David North, *August 1993*

HERON

As evening falls the black silhouette of a lone Heron flapping heavily, but purposefully to its night-time roost in the marshes, is still a common sight in Norfolk. Wherever there is water you may chance upon a Heron. Marshy meadows, rivers, ponds, salt-marshes and coastal estuaries are all suitable feeding grounds.

Outside the breeding season Herons are usually solitary, but as early as February breeding birds come together to form sometimes quite large breeding colonies, known as heronries. Some well known heronries have been used by many generations of birds. Herons build large, untidy looking nests often near the top of tall trees, and the three to five greenish eggs are laid in March.

Young Herons are comical, if somewhat ugly looking birds, with punk-like top knots of black down sticking out in all directions. The adults feed them by regurgitating partially digested food, especially fish. It is a tough life for a young Heron, and more than 70% of Herons die in their first year of life. Having survived the first difficult year there is every chance of a long life, the record age being twenty five years. At least today young Herons are no longer a favourite dish. Herons were formerly served at royal banquets, and in Norfolk Sir Thomas Browne, in the seventeenth century, writes "young hensies be esteemed a festivall dish, and much desired by some palates."

There is no mistaking a Heron whenever you see one. Of British breeding birds only swans are larger, and the combination of dagger-like bill, long neck and long legs is unmistakable. The upperparts and tail are grey, the wings grey with black flight feathers, and the underparts are white streaked black on the breast. In flight the head is hunched towards the body and the legs are extended. The loud, harsh flight call will be as familiar to fishermen as to birdwatchers.

Watching Herons requires a certain amount of patience as they will often remain standing motionless until with a sudden lightning thrust a passing fish, or even a young waterbird, is speared by that dagger-like bill. Fish, frogs, eels, small mammals, moles, rats, young Moorhens, Coots and Mallard are all favoured prey.

An unusual adaptation to this diet is their comb-like claw, used to comb a special powder through their feathers in order to clean off fish scales and slime. They produce their own "dry shampoo" from special down feathers – the Heron's "powder puff" – which crumble into a fine, absorbent cleaning powder.

Most people delight in seeing a Heron, but perhaps the pleasure may be dimmed if it is busy emptying your garden pond of goldfish! Herons can be a problem at fish farms, though you can hardly blame the Heron for calling at what must seem the avian equivalent of a MacDonald's fast food joint. The only real solution is completely caging a pond, though because Herons tend to land on the bank and then walk into the water, deep steep-sided fish ponds will prove less attractive. Lines placed around and across a pond may deter a Heron, but not if it is really hungry!

The solitary Heron, hunched motionless but observing all, is for me the perfect symbol of Norfolk's wet wildernesses.

He alights: furls his wings like a wet umbrella, settles
rapt and murderous...

Heron invented slow motion long before the movies came,
but allows himself the lightning of his pick-axe for the
killing game...

He's the hermit who daily petrifies himself in the reeds...

Heron's that sudden outlandish screech you hear at midnight
in the water meadows as he changes into the wrong gear.

FRANCIS HARVEY, Heron

JARVIS 93

AVOCET

Norfolk can be justifiably proud of its county list of breeding birds – one of the most exceptional of any county in Britain. Amongst the many bird rarities which make their home in Norfolk the Avocet must star as the most elegant and graceful. Snow white and jet black in plumage it is quite unmistakable, with its upcurved bill of exquisite fineness and striking blue-grey legs. The name Avocet is Italian in origin, and perhaps because it so much better captures the grace, beauty and sheer style of this bird it has replaced the less decorous early English names of scooper, crooked-bill and cobbler's awl. In Norfolk Avocets were also known as yarwhelps and clinkers, names probably derived from the distinctive call notes.

Many people who have never seen this bird in the wild will be familiar with the Avocet as the symbol of the Royal Society for the Protection of Birds (RSPB), Britain's premier bird protection society, and the story of this species explains why it is a true symbol of conservation success.

Avocets once nested at many sites along the English coast between Kent and the River Humber, but had become rare by the early nineteenth century. Their decline probably had many causes: both eggs and birds were taken by man as food, others were shot for sport and with rarity nests became the target for unscrupulous Victorian collectors. There are references in Victorian writings to one Salthouse gunner who regularly filled his cap, coat pockets and even his stockings with Avocet eggs for puddings and pancakes. Land reclamation and the drainage of coastal marshes for agriculture was undoubtedly also a factor in their decline, a loss of habitat which in earlier centuries had already spelt the end for other striking Norfolk birds including the Spoonbill and the Crane.

Solitary pairs of Avocets still nested in Norfolk in 1827, and perhaps in Kent until 1843, but by the 1850's Avocets were extinct in Britain as breeding birds. A whole century was to pass before, in the post-war years between 1945 and 1950, Avocets returned to nest in Suffolk. Perhaps restrictions imposed by the German occupying powers in the Netherlands during the Second World War, helped Avocet numbers to increase in Holland on undisturbed military zones, providing the impetus to allow the species to extend its range. These first Suffolk nests were carefully guarded by the RSPB, on what were later to become the famous Havergate Island and Minsmere Nature Reserves.

The first Avocets to return to Norfolk bred on Cley marshes in 1977, and since then a slow increase in numbers has allowed a further spread along the North Norfolk coast to Titchwell in 1984, and also to Holme. Whilst the great beauty and spectacle of these birds now brings enjoyment to thousands of visitors to Norfolk, sadly despite careful protection, in recent years egg collectors have succeeded in taking eggs.

Today in Norfolk the Avocet must be one of the easiest rarities to actually see, and in 1992 at least 157 pairs were presemt along the coast. A trip to the RSPB reserve at Titchwell, or the Norfolk Naturalists Trust Reserve at Cley in Summer is sure to be rewarded with views of the birds wading through shallow lagoons, picking shrimps from the brackish water with a characteristic rapid side-to-side sweeping motion of that unique upturned bill.

Careful management of these reserves controls the water levels to create just the right feeding areas for the birds, and small man-made shingle islands provide perfect nest sites. Don't leave your visit too late though, as Avocets are migrants, leaving Norfolk in September. The birds return by late February or early March, though some young birds bred on Norfolk reserves cross the North Sea to join Dutch breeding colonies.

For a really close look at Avocets a tame breeding colony has been established at the Pensthorpe Waterfowl Park near Fakenham and here birds can be viewed at close quarters throughout the year.

Wherever you choose to look for this bird your first view of an Avocet is guaranteed to be pure magic!

JARVIS '93

LAPWING

Drive anywhere in East Anglia's fenland in autumn or early winter and you won't have to travel far through the open windswept fields before you spot a field alive with Lapwings and gulls. Stop your car for a few moments and you have the ideal hide from which to watch the intriguing relationship between Black-Headed Gulls and feeding Lapwings.

The first thing you will notice is the curious way feeding Lapwings are dotted evenly across the field. Each Lapwing rather like a chess piece on its own square, maintains about a ten foot gap from its nearest neighbour. The feeding method of Lapwings is easy to observe and quite distinctive. Each bird runs rapidly forward a few steps, pauses, peers at the ground and then tips forward to peck at the ground before running on again. This "pause and run" feeding technique is characteristic of the plover family. Lapwings, sometimes known as Green Plovers, are related to shorebirds such as the Ringed and Grey Plovers which can be seen along the Norfolk coast.

Lapwings may seem a little furtive when feeding, and for good reason as dotted amongst the Lapwing flock are seagull pirates ready to steal a hungry Lapwing's food. As soon as a gull spots a Lapwing with food, it flies rapidly towards its victim. The startled Lapwing takes to the air, twisting and turning, most often dropping its food, which the gull then retrieves or catches in mid-air. This "food piracy" by gulls is technically known as kleptoparasitism.

Lapwings are beautiful birds, familiar to most Norfolk country dwellers and much liked. Seen closely the upperparts shine a glossy green with hints of purples and blues as the feathers catch the light. In the distance, however, the birds appear black and white. Both males and females have a whispy crest, though in the breeding season males can be picked out with markedly larger crests, and more contrasting black and white face markings. In flight flocks of Lapwings are unmistakable, their wings flashing alternately black above and white below. Even the call is a distinctive "pee-o-wit", from which the widely used name of peewit originates. This rather plaintive call is mentioned in the folktale which describes a Lapwing mocking Christ at the crucifixion, and condemned afterwards to live homeless, calling sorrowfully in its wanderings. In contrast the Latin name, Vanellus, means "little fan", from the throbbing sound made by the male's wings, as it tumbles in Spring display flight. The English name Lapwing itself originates from the Old English leapewince, meaning a "leap with a waver in it", the perfect description of the Lapwing's tremulous flight.

Peak numbers of Lapwings usually occur in Norfolk between October and December, when local populations are swelled by large numbers of migrants which have crossed the North Sea. Large flocks often gather on airfields and can, like gulls, prove a hazard to aircraft.

At the onset of cold weather it is common to see Lapwings passing in twinkling black and white flocks high overhead. Lapwings rely on soft ground which they can probe for insect food. Prolonged frosts bring about "hard weather movements", with birds first deserting inland fields for coastal areas and then, if cold weather persists, moving onward, both south and west.

Birds ringed in Norfolk as youngsters have been found as far south as Spain. Indeed the Spanish name for Lapwing is "Avefria" meaning "bird of the cold", reflecting the weather which often follows the arrival of these birds. On occasions Lapwings moving westward into Ireland have been caught in gales, and it is testament to their powers of flight that some survive to arrive exhausted on the shores of eastern Canada.

Though fortunately still a familiar sight in Norfolk during the autumn and winter, numbers of breeding Lapwings have seriously declined. The days when one person could collect 1900 Lapwing eggs from Norfolk marshes in a single breeding season, as was done in 1921, are long gone. The Lapwing, or Plovers' eggs, were then sold as a local delicacy until the 1926 'Lapwing Act' fortunately restricted egg collecting.

In contrast today the decline of Lapwings results from modern farming methods. Many favoured grassland breeding areas in Norfolk have been ploughed, wet hollows crucial to the survival of chicks have been drained, and the increase in the sowing of winter wheat results in a crop too tall in spring to provide the open habitat Lapwings require for nesting.

Despite these pressures there are still many Norfolk fields, especially along the coast, where in early spring the wild tumbling, zig-zags, somersaults and twists of Lapwings in display flight delight the eye, and where their wild, haunting calls ring over the marshes.

JARVIS'93

BITTERN

The Bittern is a mysterious, elusive and solitary bird – a reed-wraith, shapeshifter and ventriloquist that haunts one of our wildest and most impenetrable habitats: large, wet reedbeds.

The Bittern is an ancient inhabitant of our country – neolithic Bitterns have been preserved in peat through millennia, only to be unearthed with the destruction of their land by modern peat extraction. Like their wetland habitat, they are today in decline across Europe. The booming of the Bittern must, in former centuries, have been a familiar sound to fenland dwellers, and the numerous allusions to the bird in the poetry of the past attest to this.

The Bittern was once known as the "boom bird" or "bog drum" and, more recently, along the Suffolk coast fog horns were referred to as "sea bitterns". It is not surprising that such an elusive bird took its name not from its plumage, but from the breeding "song" of the male. The Guinness Book of Records claims the Bittern's voice as both the lowest pitched, and furthest carrying of any bird in the world. On occasion its voice is reputed to have been heard from over three miles away. Even its Latin name Botaurus, stems from "boatum tauri" – the bellowing of a bull.

Bitterns belong to the Heron family, but in comparison with our familiar Grey Heron they have shorter necks, shorter thicker legs, and are better camouflaged. Their plumage is the golden-brown colour of dead reeds in sunlight, mottled and barred with black. The bill is long and pointed, and their huge feet are coloured green. Those who are lucky enough to have watched them regularly all comment on how the Bittern can change its shape more completely than any other bird, transmuting from heavy, thickset hunchbacks prowling the marshes into scraggy things of astonishing length when they freeze in alarm. The Bittern has mastery of all the arts of concealment, and when disturbed or threatened, its neck is elongated with bill pointing skywards, whilst the eyes are swivelled downwards allowing it to peer straight forward looking round and under its bill while remaining motionless. It is even said on windy days to sway its body in rhythm to the movements of the reeds!

Male Bitterns boom between February and June. It used to be thought that to make this extraordinary low-pitched noise the Bittern pushed its bill into a reed and then blew down it like a trumpet. While the resonant booming is not particularly loud, its very low pitch gives it remarkable carrying power, and at the same time the bird remains almost impossible to locate, its voice seeming to have the same strength whether the bird is near or far away.

Legend associates the Bittern with the 'night raven' of mythology, and its voice is heard as much by night as by day. To hear the booming was said to be bad luck, though for any birdwatcher today it's a real treat!

The Bittern has a great fondness for eels and is adapted in several ways for taking this prey. The bill is serrated near its tip, enabling it to hold the slippery eels. Killing an eel is a time consuming, messy process which leaves the head and neck of the Bittern bedraggled and matted with slime. Like its cousin the Heron, the Bittern has "powder puffs" on its breast which produce a soft, downy material which breaks into minute absorbent particles of "dust". Birds can become so slimy after feeding on eels that preening lasts several hours. First the Bittern wipes its head and neck over the powder puffs; then the middle toe, which is serrated with 36 fine teeth, is used to comb out the powder and slime. After this the feathers are carefully oiled from the preen gland at the base of the tail to maintain their essential waterproofing.

Norfolk is traditionally the stronghold of Bitterns in this country, but sadly the boom bird is no longer commonly heard. In the early 19th century Bitterns were still common enough to be regarded as a delicacy, roasted for Sunday lunch, and special shoots were organised in the fens and broadlands. Sir Thomas Browne, writing of Norfolk in the 17th century, compares Herons and Bitterns saying "the bittern is also common and esteemed the better dish". A combination of shooting, egg collecting and taxidermy brought about their extinction as a British breeding bird in the 1860s. From the 1900s Bitterns boomed again in the Broads, and in 1911 young were found at Sutton Broad. Numbers slowly increased with Suffolk being colonised in 1929, and by the late 1950s they bred in seven English counties with a population of 90 pairs, 60 of which were in Norfolk. Sadly, since the early 1960s the species has again declined with only three booming males remaining in the whole of the Norfolk Broads in 1987. In 1992 there were just 20 booming males in Britain, of which only seven individuals were in Norfolk.

The reasons for this decline are complex. In the Broads, pollution and disturbance are certainly factors, but even on reedbed nature reserves the bird is disappearing. It will be a sad day if Bitterns again cease to boom in Norfolk and this time, as the species is becoming increasingly rare across Europe, recolonisation from abroad is unlikely to occur. Perhaps the Bittern is sadly a bird out of time with our modern world, but if we do lose the Bittern a little magic will die with them, and our Norfolk reedbeds will be somehow less mysterious and poorer for their passing.

In some small reedy bed . . .
The buzzing bittern sits, which through his hollow bill
A sudden bellowing sends, which many times doth fill
The neighbouring marsh with noise as though a bull did roar
Michael Drayton (1563-1631), Polyolbion

JARVIS '93

BEARDED TIT

The Bearded Tit is not well named, neither having a beard nor being a tit. In fact, the bird is closely related to the Asian and Middle Eastern babblers, rather than the tit family. The traditional Norfolk names of reed pheasant and reedling are much more descriptive of this attractive inhabitant of coastal and Broadland reed-beds than its official name.

The male is a strikingly beautiful bird, and with a blue-grey head, yellow bill and long, black tapering moustache he really can't be mistaken for any other bird. The female is duller, being a warm, reedy-brown all over with darker markings on her tail and wings. However, the long, graduated tail, about three inches in length, and the lack of any streaking on breast and back distinguishes her from a female Reed Bunting, the only other bird which, when fleetingly glimpsed among the reed stems, she could be confused with. The soft, warm browns, greys and buffs of both sexes match them perfectly to the colours of their reed-bed haunts

Bearded Tits have probably never been common in England, and Norfolk and Suffolk have always been the stronghold of this species. Early in the nineteenth century Bearded Tits were fairly widespread in southern and eastern England, but the Victorian fondness for egg collecting and taxidermy, together with the drainage of many reed beds, caused a decline throughout this period. Arthur Patterson in "Wildlife on a Norfolk Estuary" (1906), quotes the following letter "Dear Sir, Could you get me bearded tits in the flesh? Can give you 3s 6d each. Also nests and eggs of same." Throughout the 1800s eggs were ruthlessly taken by fenmen to be sold for as much as four shillings a dozen, with live birds taken in nets or on limed sticks fetching five shillings a pair. It is hardly surprising when a day's 'egging' brought in more money than a day's work that the birds were ruthlessly persecuted. Fortunately, because of grave concern that any birds at all would survive, some legal protection was given to the species in 1895.

The other main threat to the reedling has always been hard winters. The winters of 1916/17, 1939/40 and 1946/47 quite literally decimated populations and it is suggested that only 10 pairs remained in England, confined to Norfolk and Suffolk, by the summer of 1947. Riviere, in his "History of Norfolk Birds", states that in 1930 the principal breeding areas were along the River Bure Valley and at Hickling Broad, Horsey Mere, Ranworth and Hoveton with a total population of perhaps 30 pairs.

From the 1950s numbers began to increase markedly, and during the 1960s and early 1970s there was definite evidence that colonisation of birds from the Netherlands occurred. The vast reed-beds established during the reclamation programme of the Zuider Zee (Ijsselmeer) supported substantial populations of Bearded Tits, and ringing recoveries have proved that some birds made the North Sea crossing to Norfolk.

Even without immigration from continental populations Bearded Tits have a remarkable ability to recover in numbers after hard winters. A single pair can rear three broods over a summer, with a typical clutch being between five and eight eggs. The nest is built at the base of the reeds, loosely woven from reed and sedge and lined with the feathery, silver heads of the reed. Both young and adults feed on insects during the summer, but change their habits in the winter becoming seed-eaters, feeding mainly on the seeds of the common reed (phragmites) but also on willowherb and nettle seeds.

It requires both luck and patience to observe Bearded Tits closely. Some days they can prove frustratingly elusive, while on other occasions they are confident and apparently tame. Their wings whirr in a blur of motion as they zip like tiny pheasants over the reed tops. In spring, pairs perform light, dancing flights, rising and dipping above the reed stems swaying in the wind, and sometimes, with a foot on two separate reeds, appear to be doing the splits.

In spring the males sometimes fight furiously, with their soft feathers fluffed out making them look twice their normal size, grey head feathers held erect and the black moustache flaunted. During courtship the male's tail is frequently flicked up and down revealing a jet black area underneath. Pairs will sometimes sit snuggled together on a reed with the male raising one wing over his mate; the picture of conjugal bliss.

The best places to observe this reed sprite are Cley and Titchwell on the North Norfolk coast, and in the Norfolk Broads at the Norfolk Naturalists Trust reserves of Ranworth and Hickling. However, in the autumn, when birds perform short exploratory journeys, visit any large reed bed in Norfolk and you could be fortunate enough to observe Bearded Tits.

Today, the vulnerability of this species is more due to its total dependence on suitable reed-bed habitat than on other threats from mankind. The population remains probably fewer than 100 pairs in Norfolk, and could still be seriously threatened by a series of bad winters. Its future will depend on the active management of reserves such as Cley, Titchwell and Hickling to maintain an abundance of reed-beds. These areas, without management, would eventually turn into wet alder and willow woodland, rather than the reedy wilderness on which the Bearded Tit depends.

JARVIS.'93

MARSH HARRIER

Norfolk can be proud of being a stronghold for three very special, and very different reedbed birds – the Bittern, the Bearded Tit and our only marshland bird of prey, the Marsh Harrier. The Norfolk Broads and reedbeds along the North Norfolk coast such as at Cley, Titchwell, Holkham and Burnham Overy are excellent sites to look for this spectacular marshland bird.

Even at a distance Marsh Harriers are very distinctive. They most often fly with a characteristic series of heavy flaps followed by gliding with wings held raised in a shallow "v". When hunting over reedbeds or dense marshland vegetation they will fly low and into the wind. This reduces their ground speed, which is doubtless helpful when looking for prey amongst tall vegetation. The curious arrangement of the face feathers, which gives them an almost owl-like mask, probably functions to funnel sound to their highly sensitive ears. This is another adaptation to finding prey in dense cover. Favoured prey includes water voles, Moorhens, Coots, the eggs and young of other birds, frogs, grass snakes and, of course, the occasional duck if they can surprise one. Rather surprisingly a study of Marsh Harriers breeding at Titchwell showed their favourite food to be juvenile Starlings and young rabbits, so there is obviously considerable variation in the diet of individual birds.

The plumage of both sexes is attractive. Though the female is basically dark brown, her crown, throat and forewings are light, sometimes golden-yellow, sometimes creamy-white. The male is the only harrier in Britain to show black-tipped wings with grey wing panels contrasting with a reddish-brown body.

April and May are two of the most exciting months to watch Marsh Harriers, as there is always a chance of seeing the male's spectacular aerial courtship displays. The male bird will fly high above the female calling plaintively "kee-oo, kee-oo" before tumbling and sometimes even somersaulting in what appears to be an uncontrollable dive towards the ground. At the last minute, in true air-display style, he will pull out of the dive and perhaps even loop-the-loop as he again heads skywards. These spring displays are known as "sky dances" and flaunt the male's silver-grey and brown wings to best effect for the female below.

The large, untidy nest is built entirely by the female, who alone incubates her three to six eggs for around 40 days before they hatch. Indeed some, usually older, males are polygamous, mating with two females, and sometimes bringing food to both nests. During incubation the male visits the nesting area two or three times a day. He calls the female off the nest and food is passed from male to female in mid-air. This food pass demonstrates the Harrier's flying ability to the full. The female sometimes flips upside down as she takes the food from the male's talons, or sometimes catches food in mid-air after the male has dropped it.

Peak numbers of Marsh Harriers are to be seen in August, by which time the youngsters and adults will be flying together. At this time of year, communal roosts have been recorded in arable fields with up to 30 individuals at one roost-site. By late September most birds have departed on a migration which will take some individuals to the tropics of Africa. British ringed birds have been recovered in Senegal and Mauritania. Doubtless many Norfolk-bred birds will die running the gauntlet of guns in southern Europe. The ratio of birdwatchers to hunters in France and Italy has been estimated at, respectively, 1:1,050 and 1:22,300! A few birds, usually females and immatures, don't migrate and will over-winter in the Norfolk Broads, joining communal roosts with Hen Harriers and Merlins.

The Marsh Harrier has not always been a rare bird. At the beginning of the last century it still bred in many counties of England and Wales. Sadly by the end of that century, like the Bittern and the Avocet, it was extinct as a British breeding bird, largely through overzealous game-keeping and the depredations of Victorian collectors.

In 1911 Marsh Harriers returned to breed in the Norfolk Broads, but by 1958 there were still only 15 pairs confined to Norfolk and Suffolk. A serious decline in numbers took place throughout the 1960s and by 1971 only a single pair still bred in England on the famous RSPB reserve at Minsmere. This decline was certainly caused, in part, by toxic farm pesticides which resulted in egg-thinning and breeding failure. Increased numbers of coypu in the Broads may also have badly affected the population there.

The 1980s saw a remarkable upturn in the fortunes of this bird, and today Norfolk's population of Marsh Harriers is higher than at any previous time this century. Many reedbed areas where the bird breeds are now well protected as nature reserves, but it is also very encouraging that Marsh Harriers have adapted to nesting in cereal fields. 1982 saw the first recorded nesting by a Marsh Harrier in Norfolk in an arable crop, and today over 25 per cent of the nesting population use this habitat. Most encouraging of all, despite the obvious dangers from farm work such as spraying and harvesting, the survival rate of young from these farmland nests has been very high. This is solely due to the care and pride of individual farmers and contractors who mark the nests and take steps to protect the birds.

Surely this represents a most encouraging change in the attitude of Norfolk landowners both to birds in general and to birds of prey in particular. Your chances of watching the "sky dancer" this spring have never been better at any time this century.

JARVIS '93

OYSTERCATCHER

The Norfolk coastline with its saltmarshes and estuaries is a wonderful area for studying wading birds. Amongst our shore birds none draws attention to itself quite so much as the conspicuous and noisy Oystercatcher. Many waders are difficult to identify, but the boldly patterned black and white Oystercatcher, with its bright orange bill, is unmistakable.

Seen closely it has a striking red eye and sturdy pink legs and feet. In flight the broad white wing bar and white rump contrast dramatically with the black of head, neck and back. The tail is edged with a broad black band. In winter plumage, many birds sport a rather clerical-looking white half-collar around their necks.

The easiest time to see Oystercatchers is in the winter, when tens of thousands of migratory birds come to Norfolk. The Wash alone may hold between 20,000 and 30,000 bird: nearly 10% of the British wintering population. Bird ringing has shown that many of these birds are from breeding grounds along the west coast of Norway. One of the best places to see these huge wintering flocks is at the Snettisham RSPB reserve, where on high tides they roost on shingle spits in front of the public hides.

In summer, numbers are tiny in comparison, with only a few hundred pairs breeding in Norfolk at sites such as Blakeney Point, Morston and Holkham marshes. However, non-breeding adults can be seen almost anywhere along the coast where there are suitable feeding grounds. A recent trend has been for birds to nest inland. Old gravel workings, such as those at Pensthorpe Waterfowl Park near Fakenham, always support a few nesting pairs, and even arable fields may be used. At inland nesting sites birds return to take up their territories as early as the end of February, and the noisy pipings of newly arrived birds is a welcome sign that winter's end is not far away.

Oystercatchers are specialised feeders, though their name is somewhat of a misnomer, and few birdwatchers will ever have seen an Oystercatcher eating oysters. Perhaps, as in the days of Dickens when oysters were a poor man's food, and huge natural oysterbeds still existed, then Oystercatchers may have eaten oysters. The older names of mussel picker and mussel cracker are more accurate, and in Norfolk the name sea pie was descriptive of the bird's bold black and white plumage. Their fondness for shellfish – especially cockles and mussels – makes Oystercatchers unique among waders in being considered a serious pest to the shellfish industry.

Feeding times are determined more by the tides than by daylight, and many birds will continue feeding after dark. An individual Oystercatcher can eat 280 cockles per tide, and up to 150 times its own weight a year! Some cockles and mussels are opened by first snipping apart the muscle which holds the shell firmly shut, and then prising it open with the tip of the bill. Other birds simply use their powerful bills to hammer the shell open, the mud around being strewn with broken and empty shells. Personal preferences in feeding techniques are passed on from parent to chick.

One of the delights of watching Oystercatchers is their range of displays. On the breeding grounds they have a wonderful, ritualised "piping" display. This can involve anything up to seven or eight individual birds which point their heads and bills straight downwards and prance about like clockwork toys, piping constantly. They also have a beautiful "butterfly" display flight, flying with deep, slow wing beats, while whistling noisily.

The eggs, laid in a simple scrape, are well camouflaged, usually a light buffish brown in colour, streaked, spotted and stippled darker brown or black.

Though on hatching the chicks quickly leave the nest site, adult Oystercatchers are unusual among waders in carrying food to their chicks. The chicks will take many weeks to learn all the specialised techniques of hammering limpets from rocks and opening cockle and mussel shells.

Wherever and whenever you watch Oystercatchers you cannot help being impressed by their vitality and excitement. A walk along our coast wouldn't be the same without the accompaniment of their noisy pipings.

JARVIS '93

RUFF

The Ruff is one of Britain's rarest breeding birds, and is most commonly seen when birds on migration pass through this country. Along the North Norfolk coast this elegant wader is not an uncommon sight during spring and autumn. At sites such as Holme, Titchwell, Holkham and Cley groups of 20 or 30 can often be seen.

The name "ruff" derives from the remarkable Elizabethan-style ruff, or frill, of feathers round the neck of the male during the breeding season. From late April to July each male bird can be individually recognised by its colours, which range from white through reddish browns to orange and even black.

On the breeding grounds, the males gather at traditional sites known as "leks", where they display and fight. They pose with heads down and ruffs extended, each male defending a territory just two or three feet across. Only the dominant males will mate with the much smaller females, known as "Reeves," and after mating the Reeve alone finds a nesting site, incubates her four eggs, and rears the young.

By autumn most Ruff are basically brown, and at a distance might be confused with the more common Redshank, though the neck is longer and the bill shorter. In all plumages, the buff edging to feathers on the back gives a characteristic scaly or scalloped appearance, which distinguishes the Ruff from other similar sized waders.

In former centuries Ruff would have been a widespread breeding species among the fen meadows and marshland of Norfolk. In the seventeenth century Sir Thomas Browne gave an excellent description of the species: "Ruffes a marsh bird of the greatest varietie of colours every one therein somewhat varying from other. The female is called a Reeve without any ruffe about the neck, lesser than the other and hardly to be got. They most abound in Marshland, butt are also in good number in the marshes between Norwich and Yarmouth."

Another seventeenth century observer, John Ray, describes how Ruff were caught in the fenlands. "They breed in summertime in the Fens of Lincolnshire about Crowland. They are fatted with white bread and milk, like Knots, being shut up in close dark rooms. For let in but the light upon them, presently they fall a fighting, never giving over till one hath killed the other, especially if anybody stand by. The Fowlers when they see them intent upon fighting, spread their nets over them, and catch them before they be aware.

In the Spring time they come over also to the Low countries: And it is reported that at the first coming in the beginning of Spring there are many more Cocks than Hens, but that they never cease fighting till there be so many Cocks killed, as to make the number of both sexes equal."

The Latin name for Ruff, Philomachus pugnax, bears out Ray's description of fighting Ruffs. In Greek, philos means "lover" and mache means "fight", and pugnax is the Latin word from which pugnacious is derived.

So common were Ruffs during the sixteenth and seventeenth centuries that even on the outskirts of Norwich they were netted alive, put in cages and fattened up on boiled wheat. They would then be killed and sold as a food delicacy on the Cambridge, Peterborough and Norwich markets, and were even exported to London.

Birds are especially good indicators of environmental change, and the demise of the Ruff as a breeding species reflects the drainage of the wet grassland and fen meadow habitat, which formerly were its breeding grounds. Ruffs ceased to breed in England in the 1870s, the last few birds being hastened to extinction through egg collecting, shooting and taxidermy. In 1968 Ruffs again bred in East Anglia, and since then a handful of pairs have attempted to nest most years, at sites such as Welney on the Ouse Washes. Fortunately, today these sites are well protected as nature reserves.

The Ruffs seen in Norfolk during late summer and autumn are mainly migratory birds from breeding sites on the Arctic and sub-Arctic tundra of Europe and Asia. Birds from the north and east pass through Norfolk on a journey which will take some of them along the Atlantic coasts of France, Spain and Portugal and thence through Africa to winter on the shores of Lake Chad.

JARVIS '92

WOODCOCK

The Woodcock is a mysterious bird. Our only woodland wader, it has deserted the marshes and wetlands favoured by other wading birds, and taken up a secretive and solitary existence in the hidden world of our woodlands.

It is not surprising that the presence of Woodcock in Norfolk's woodlands is often overlooked. Its beautifully marked russet-brown, black, grey and buff feathering render it almost invisible against a background of dead leaves and bracken. Woodcock rely on this superb camouflage to escape detection, and will crouch rather than fly, only springing into the air at the last moment from almost under your feet. Its erratic dodging and weaving flight between trees and shrubs make it a challenging target for the sportsman. A right and left at a Woodcock is one of the most sought-after achievements in the sporting world, and special Woodcock shoots are organised during the winter.

The Woodcock's favourite prey is earthworms, which it deftly extracts from the damp woodland soil with a specially adapted long, blunt-ended bill. Even when probing the ground the large, dark eyes placed high up on the sides of the head allow the bird almost 360 degrees vision, and it is constantly alert for danger from a passing fox or Sparrowhawk.

During the winter time this secretive bird is more widely distributed in Norfolk than many birdwatchers realise. Even small spinneys can hold birds. In early winter large numbers of Woodcock may suddenly arrive along the east coast of Great Britain. These will be birds from Russia, Scandinavia, Germany and Holland, which are forced to migrate as soon as bad weather and frosts render the ground too hard for a Woodcock to probe. A fall of Woodcock along the coast brings birds to sand dunes and open country where they are more easily spotted than in their usual woodland habitat.

The other time of year when Woodcock are most likely to be seen is during the breeding season when the males perform a strange display flight known as "roding". The unusual grunting display call, followed by a whistling "tsiwick", will draw your attention to birds flying just above the tree canopy at dusk and dawn. This display flight occurs between February and June – an extended season because males are polygamous and having mated with one female will continue roding in the hope of attracting further mates.

One of the enigmas associated with breeding Woodcock is whether they are able to carry their young in flight. Charles St John, in 1848, first described this behaviour which, if true, is unique to Woodcock. Doubtless until the behaviour is photographed or filmed the controversy will continue.

GREAT CRESTED GREBE

Perhaps the best area in Norfolk to look for this exotic looking bird is the Norfolk Broads, Almost every Broad can boast one or more pairs. Away from the Broads older gravel pits, or the ornamental lakes of large estates, provide good breeding sites for this species.

The fortunes of this spectacular bird have been intimately linked to human activities. During the last century the Great Crested Grebe was persecuted for its feathers, which were used in the fashion industry. In the mid 1840's skins were fetching 10 shillings a time and were in high demand for ladies' muffs and stoles. By the 1860's only around 40 pairs remained in England, and pressure from early conservationists forced the passing of the Seabirds Protection Act through Parliament in 1869. This stopped the slaughter of the few remaining birds. Since then, the population of Great Crested Grebes has increased to over 2000 pairs, benefiting this century from the creation of new lakes formed from old gravel workings and quarrying.

Grebes are superbly adapted to their aquatic lifestyle and seem almost more at home under the water than on the surface. Their legs are placed so far towards the rear of the body that they are useless for walking, but perfect, with their flattened sides and broad lobed toes, for propelling the bird torpedo-like under the water in search of fish.

Spring is the most exciting time to watch Great Crested Grebes. Courtship displays are complex and involve head shaking, with pairs facing each other with the neck ruff of feathers extended. Prior to mating a special floating reed platform is built which the birds then use for mating. Later this may be built up to form the nest, or a separate floating nest is built nearby.

The 3 to 6 chalky-white eggs hatch after 30 days, and then the downy grey and black striped young can be seen being carried over the water on their parents' backs. Close observation of grebes feeding young or preening will reveal one of their stranger habits – feather eating. Small feathers, from the grebe's breast are fed to their young, and are also eaten by the adults themselves. It is thought that the plug of feathers which builds up in the stomach may help with regurgitating fish bones or even protect birds from intestinal parasites, such as tape-worms and flukes.

Today the Great Crested Grebe, whilst protected from its earlier problems of hunting and shooting, faces the more modern threat of pollution. A bird so totally dependent on water is at risk from oil spills at sea in winter, and in summer from the widespread problem of deteriorating water quality and pesticide pollution. Sadly many nests in the Norfolk Broads are lost each summer, swamped by the wash of passing motor boats, their drivers oblivious to this beauty hidden in the reeds.

MUTE SWAN

Britain's largest bird, larger than a Golden Eagle and one of the heaviest flying birds in the world, is fortunately also one of our tamest birds. There can be few children who at some time haven't been taken to feed the swans on their local river or pond. Next to the Robin, the Mute Swan must surely be our best known British bird.

Swans are widely distributed on rivers, estuaries, ponds, lakes and streams, the only restriction being the requirement for at least 20 metres open water for take-off, which can only be achieved by pattering along the surface whilst flapping the wings furiously.

During the winter Mute Swans can be mistaken for their migratory cousins, the Whooper and Bewick's Swans. However, at close quarters the orange and black bill of the Mute is very different from the yellow and black bills of the other species, and its neck is more gracefully curved.

The name "Mute" is something of a misnomer, as a whole range of grunts, growls, hisses and yaps are made by the adults and the young cygnets also have a piping whistle to help the parents maintain contact with them. In flight the rhythmic throbbing of the wings is distinctive, and probably assists swans flying at night, or in the mist, to maintain contact with each other.

The breeding season begins early, and by February the cob, recognised by the large knob on his bill, will be patrolling his chosen territory. To drive away intruders, the wings will be arched over the back, neck feathers ruffled out, and he will surge forward looking most intimidating. It is always wise to keep well away from angry swans, but although the wings can occasionally strike a heavy painful blow, their strength has been much exaggerated.

The nest is built at the water's edge by both birds, but only the pen will incubate the six, or sometimes more, large eggs.The cygnets hatch after 36 days, and for the first few weeks of life are often carried on their parents' backs.This keeps the cygnets warm, and protects them from pike, which are quite capable of taking a cygnet in its first few days. Sadly many cygnets die during their second week of life as the nourishment originally obtained from the yolk sac is used up.

For older birds, power lines are one of the major hazards, with many hundreds of swans dying each year through collisions. In the recent past lead poisoning was probably the single biggest cause of death among swans, with an estimated 4,000 birds dying annually. The swans eat anglers' discarded split lead shot, mistaking it for the grit which is needed in their gizzards to grind up their food. In January 1987 a ban on the sale of the smaller sized angler's weights was introduced, and this together with the introduction of non-toxic substitutes has considerably helped the situation. Even so, it is likely that more than half of all swans die from man-made causes, whether tangled up in litter or fishing line, oiled, or perhaps saddest of all, the victims of deliberate brutality.

Swans have always been symbols of purity, though the common belief that swans mate for life and are faithful to their partners isn't entirely true. Modern studies have shown that divorce occurs in at least 10 per cent of pairs. Many myths and stories have arisen about swans, and their scientific name "Cygnus" is of Greek origin. Cygnus was the son of Apollo, and both he and his mother were transformed into swans after leaping to their deaths in a lake. The constellation Cygnus is also one of the brightest star groups in the night sky, and, with an imaginative eye, does resemble a flying swan. A widespread myth in Europe is the story of the swan maidens. These attractive maidens were really swans, but could be captured and married if their feathery cloaks were seized and hidden.

In the past, swans in England were valuable property. From the thirteenth century until the eighteenth all swans were the property of the Crown, except those granted by licence to others, which were marked with a notch in the bill, or the web of the foot. The Walpole family of the Mannington estate had their own swan mark. "Swan-upping" was the annual round-up of swans, and strict rules were followed to determine ownership of cygnets. If the parent birds had the marks of two different owners, then half the cygnets went to each, though often a "ground bird", a single cygnet, was given to the landowner where they had nested. Today, the tradition continues on the Thames where an annual swan-upping is still held, and birds are marked for the Queen and Worshipful Companies of Vintners and Dyers. Mute Swans were of course eaten regularly in former centuries. Cygnets were taken from their parents at about three months, and put in special pits to be fattened for Christmas. There was a certain snob value in eating swans; roast swan for the upper classes, and goose for the lower. It is recorded that Henry III had 125 swans roasted for the Court Christmas dinner in 1251, and when the Archbishop of York was installed in 1466, 400 were eaten!

JARVIS.

PINK-FOOTED GOOSE

Pink-footed Geese, or "Pinkfeet" as they are commonly called, occur along the Norfolk coast in winter in huge numbers. In the winter of 1990-91 Norfolk held 20 per cent of the world population of this species.

Pinkfeet are the most numerous geese on the Norfolk coast, but are shyer and less often seen closely than the smaller, darker Brent. Their plumage is basically brown with a noticeably darker head and neck, and rather attractive white edging to the wing feathers. The characteristic bill pattern and pink legs distinguish them from similar "grey geese" such as Whitefronts and Beans.

Over the last 10 years numbers have increased in north Norfolk from about 4,000 to some 20,000 geese. There are three main winter roosts: the vast open mud-flats of the Wash, Scolt Head Island, and the sands off the isolated East Hills at Wells. In total some 195,000 Pinkfeet winter in Britain, with the rest of the world's population, some 30,000 birds, wintering in the Netherlands and Belgium. Norfolk lies at the southern end of a migration route which brings Pinkfeet from Iceland and Greenland. High counts in Norfolk usually follow severe weather in the north of England, when feeding grounds there are snow-covered or frozen hard.

The feeding habits of Pinkfeet in Norfolk have been intensively studied by the University of East Anglia. What has been discovered is that on arrival in late October and November, the geese favour stubble fields where waste grain has germinated providing tender young shoots, or where spilt grain remains. Even more delicious to the palate of a hungry Pink-footed Goose are the leaves and roots of sugar beet, especially the discarded sprouting beet tops. Sugar beet is perhaps the major food source for Pinkfeet wintering in Norfolk, though cereal, potato and carrot fields are also visited, especially later in the season.

Large flocks of Pinkfeet feeding on the tender young shoots of winter cereals is understandably not a welcome sight to farmers, and a variety of techniques, from bird scarers and scarecrows to shooting, are used to move the birds on. Geese damage crops in two main ways: by feeding and by trampling. A thousand pairs of Pinkfeet, each bird weighing a hefty five or six pounds, will soon puddle the surface of a wet, ploughed field, which will then dry to a hard-pan of mud, not very condusive to good crop growth. On the other hand, damage by feeding on crops is perhaps less severe than it might first appear. Shoots are torn off with the cutting edge of the side of that short, stubby pink and black bill, but the roots are left undamaged, often resulting in the plant putting up two new shoots where only one grew before. It is also true that an actively feeding goose produces a dropping every three minutes, so a flock of 1,000 Pinkfeet, grazing for several hours, will add a vast weight of free fertilizer, rich in nitrates and phosphates, to the crop. But then I'm a great admirer of all geese, and I'm sure others might be less charitable in their analysis of the damage!

Hopefully the Ministry of Agriculture's new set-aside scheme will solve some of the problems, as in Norfolk's coastal areas farmers can gain additional payments by managing set-aside land specifically to attract wintering geese.

Anyone who walks the north Norfolk coast in winter will have enjoyed their clamorous calls, and the magic of skein after skein of geese passing overhead, or "whiffling" – those characteristic and very beautiful erratic side-to-side aerobatics done by geese as they lose height rapidly, before landing.

But where do our geese go each summer? The answer has been found largely from bird-ringing studies. It was the late Sir Peter Scott who, in 1951, discovered the Pinkfeet's main breeding site at Thjorsarver in Iceland. This summer home is a strange, lunar-looking volcanic desert, its landscape gouged by glaciers and formed by vast lava-flows. Pinkfeet nest here on inaccessible crags in deep gorges, and their day-old goslings are led on an incredible journey across this barren landscape to small islands of dwarf, heathy vegetation which serve as gosling nurseries. Breeding success is almost entirely dependent on favourable weather, and a late thaw of the snows, delaying the breeding season, can mean virtually no young are produced. The majority of Norfolk's wintering geese originate from breeding sites in Iceland, though some Pinkfeet wintering in Britain have an even more arduous migration from the east of Greenland. The birds wintering in Belgium and the Netherlands are an entirely separate population, breeding in Spitzbergen.

The arrival and departure of the Pinkfeet from Norfolk each autumn and spring never ceases to thrill. Countless Norfolk wildfowlers will have tales to tell of cold, misty dawns on the Norfolk coast when the Pinkfeet are flighting low enough for the chance of a shot. Next time you see a skein of Pinkfeet passing overhead, travel with them and imagine the strange lava landscapes of Iceland which are as familiar to them as a beet field in north Norfolk.

JARVIS '92

BRENT GOOSE

For some 12,000 Brent Geese, Norfolk is the last stop on a 2-3,000 mile journey; a migration which has taken them from the high Arctic tundra of Russia's Western Siberia, along the Baltic shores of Finland and Denmark, and finally across the North Sea from the Netherlands to the salt marshes which fringe the Norfolk coast.

The Russian, or dark bellied Brent Geese, leave their northern breeding grounds in August and early September, arriving in Norfolk during October and November. Brent are the smallest British geese, little larger than a drake Mallard, and easily recognised by their generally dark appearance with all-black heads, necks and upper breasts. At close range a thin, white half-collar is visible on the neck and in flight their sterns gleam white in contrast to their dark bodies. The name Brent, or Brant Goose as they are known in North America, originates from the old Norse "brandgas", meaning burnt goose, descriptive of their charcoal-black plumage.

In autumn and early winter, when flocks of Brent first return to Norfolk, most of their time is spent on salt marshes, mudflats, sandbanks and estuaries. Locally they are referred to as "Sea Geese". from their habit of spending more time on and near the sea than any other species of goose. Indeed, highly developed salt glands enable them to consume saline saltmarsh plants, and even to drink seawater.

One of their staple foods is eel grass which grows on tidal mudflats. During the 1920's and 30's a wasting disease affected the growth of eel grass, and with the decline in food supply the world population of Russian Brent Geese crashed to around 16,500. Because of this severe decline, protection from shooting was given to Brent Geese in 1954, and since then the population has increased.

Today, England is winter home to around 90,000 Russian Brent Geese, roughly half the world population. This recent increase in numbers has led to pressure from wildfowlers to reinstate Brent Geese as a legitimate quarry species. Last century Brent Geese were a favourite target for wildfowlers; in 1860 at Dengie in Essex 32 punt-gunners firing together brought down 704 Brent, not taking into account injured birds.

Many Norfolk farmers are none too happy with the increased numbers of birds because in recent years Brent Geese have changed their feeding habits and now, especially in late winter, move behind the sea wall to feed on arable crops and pasture grass.

Between November and March it is fairly easy to see Brent Geese in Norfolk; Blakeney, Wells, Holkham, Brancaster and the Wash coastline are all favoured sites. To watch Brent in comfort try parking on the quayside at Wells and look for small flocks of dark geese with white sterns, flying in straggly lines over the saltings, or bobbing up and down in small groups on the water at high tide.

The future for Brent Geese in Norfolk looks fairly secure as many of their favoured areas along the North Norfolk coast are now well protected as nature reserves. However, outside Norfolk many wintering areas are threatened by reclamation of estuarine land for agricultural and industrial development, port extensions, and the building of marinas.

CUCKOO

For a well known, much talked about and much loved British bird it is surprising how few people could clearly describe the Cuckoo. At a glimpse it appears hawk-like: a dark, slaty grey bird with pointed wings and a long tail. Indeed it was once a popular belief that the Cuckoo turned into a Sparrowhawk in the winter, and sadly it was not uncommon for gamekeepers to shoot Cuckoos merely upon suspicion of this being true. Hopefully we live in more enlightened times, and gamekeepers today are both more knowledgeable and more conservation-minded.

If you are lucky enough to get a close-up view of a Cuckoo, then a generally grey bird is revealed, slate grey above and barred below. The tail is long and graduated, with white tips to the tail feathers, and is often raised and lowered whilst the bird perches. Whilst its flight between trees is fast and direct, it has a rather clumsy way of moving amongst vegetation and branches with wings held half open, often seeming unbalanced in its movements.

For most of us the Cuckoo is well known not for its looks, but for its voice, which can carry for over a mile and is without doubt the most widely recognised of British bird calls. The "cuck-ooooo" call is only made by male birds, the female having a beautiful, liquid bubbling trill, which is less well known.

There is a long tradition of listening for the first Cuckoo each spring, today exemplified by that letter to "The Times". At Marsham in Norfolk there are records of each year's first Cuckoo between 1736 and 1925; the earliest recorded being on April 12th and the latest May 7th.

The unique breeding behaviour of Cuckoos is known to scientists as "obligate brood parasitism" and to the rest of us as laying eggs in the nests of other birds. The Cuckoo is the only British bird never to build a nest of its own, and the female Cuckoo carefully removes one egg from the nest of the unwilling host before laying one of her own. Common host species are Meadow Pipits, Dunnocks and Reed Warblers. Each hen Cuckoo tries to lay her eggs in nests of one species, and her eggs, though larger, often closely mimic the colour and patterning of the host bird's normal eggs. On hatching the young Cuckoo, though blind and featherless, within a few hours begins the tortuous task of heaving any eggs or young out of the nest, using a pronounced hollow on its back to raise the eggs one by one over the lip of the nest. As sole occupant of the nest it grows rapidly, vociferously demanding constant feeding. Its large red gape and constant begging calls are such powerful stimuli that sometimes other birds nesting nearby are drawn to feed young Cuckoos.

Another miracle of the Cuckoo's bizarre lifestyle is its migration. Cuckoos migrate to southern Africa for the winter, but most adult Cuckoos depart England by the end of July whilst their young are still in the nests of other birds. The young Cuckoos are mysteriously able to follow the adults on this migration months later, many not leaving England until September.

There is still much to be learned about this intriguing species, but perhaps it is only right that the Cuckoo remains, as Wordsworth described:

> *"No bird, but an invisible thing,*
> *A voice, a mystery."*

KINGFISHER

An early name for the Kingfisher was "alceon" or "halcyon", and legend had it that the Kingfisher built a floating nest on the sea during the halcyon days; a period of calm extending seven days before, and seven days after the shortest day of winter. The origin of its more recent name is literally King's Fisher, or King of the Fishers. Several legends attest to the magical properties of Kingfishers, including the power of their electric blue feathers to prevent lightning striking anyone who wears them.

The Kingfisher's colour almost defies description, and indeed depending on the angle of the light the bird's upperparts can appear from azure blue to green, or almost any shade in-between. The brightest iridescent blue is on the rump and tail, the wings and head being a darker shade of blue with a patch of chestnut and white behind the eye. The underparts are a warm chestnut orange, and the dagger-like bill is all black in the males, whereas adult females have a red lower mandible. The feet and legs are ceiling-wax red. This tropically coloured bird does indeed belong to a mainly tropical family of birds. There are about ninety species of Kingfisher in the world, occurring mainly in the Tropics, and our common Kingfisher is the most northerly representative of this group, its range extending as far north as Sweden.

Kingfishers are notoriously shy. Indeed it has been said that only the righteous ever see the Kingfisher! Righteous or not, if you are lucky enough to see the bird closely you may be surprised at its small size. Little larger than a sparrow, it measures about six inches from bill-tip to tail, yet can eat a fish up to three and a half inches long!

The Kingfisher's diet consists, mainly, though not exclusively, of small fish. Typically birds will perch on a branch overhanging the water, intently watching for movements below. A sudden plunge, straight as an arrow and almost too fast for the eye to follow, and a second later the bird is back on its perch with a minnow or stickleback.

The Kingfisher makes this feat appear simple, but remember that before the bird hits the water it has judged the depth of the water, taken into account the angle of refraction, and allowed for the movement of both the current and the fish. It has to calculate all this in advance of hitting the water as the fish is actually caught with the Kingfisher's eyes closed! On entering the water the second eyelid, or nictitating membrane, which is opaque, is pulled across the eye for protection. It is a common misconception that fish are speared, and whilst this might happen occasionally, probably in error, more normally the fish is grasped between the mandibles.

On return to its perch, different prey will be dealt with in a variety of ways. Minnows are simply nipped between the gills and swallowed headfirst, whereas with sticklebacks the fish is beaten many times against the perch to flatten the spines which otherwise could choke the bird. Kingfishers must eat at least their own weight in food every day, probably more in cold weather, and a typical day's diet might consist of seventeen or eighteen small fish.

Kingfishers are highly territorial, defending a patch of up to one mile of river. This stretch they will know better than any human fisherman. Pairs come together as early as January, and will then begin prospecting nest-sites. The nest is a chamber at the end of a slightly upward sloping tunnel in the bank of a stream. Tunnelling begins with the birds flinging themselves dartlike against the bank to loosen the soil. Once a small depression has been made they will perch, and from then on dig their way in. Soil loosened with the bill will be shovelled backwards with the feet, and finally pushed out with the tail. The finished tunnel, which may be three feet in length, is always straight allowing a little light to reach the nest chamber. This is important as the youngsters instinctively squirt their foul smelling, oily droppings toward the light and down the tunnel. With a typical brood of six or seven youngsters the tunnel soon becomes so filthy that adults will bathe after every visit to the nest.

Two or even three clutches are not uncommon in a breeding season, but many young Kingfishers will perish in the first few weeks after leaving the nest. Parents do not teach their young to catch fish, and whilst this is instinctive behaviour, their skills only improve with practice, and many birds will die, exhausted from futile dives, but driven by hunger to continue until they become waterlogged and drown.

Still other birds will die in their first winter during spells of bitter, cold weather. Prolonged freezing is obviously a major problem and although some birds will move to the coast or estuaries during cold spells, many will simply not survive. A more modern threat is pollution. The Kingfisher's natural habitat is slow moving, lowland rivers and streams with high vertical banks for nesting, and plenty of shallows fringed with overhanging trees for fishing perches. In Norfolk, as elsewhere in England, most rivers suffer some pollution, and if fish populations decline, Kingfishers too will decline.

Fortunately Kingfishers are still widespread in Norfolk, and if you join the virtuous by rising at dawn to walk a river bank there is every chance of catching a glimpse of the Fisher King about his business.

JARVIS '92

ROBIN

The Robin is perhaps the best known and most loved British bird, familiar to all and celebrated each Christmas on countless cards. Its orange-red breast is the Robin's most conspicuous feature, and it is often simply called "redbreast" or "robin redbreast". The Saxon name "ruddock", widespread in local use until the nineteenth century, also referred to the Robin's red colouring.

Robins feature in numerous myths and legends. The origin of its red-breast is said to have come about when the bird stained its feathers red with Christ's blood, as it valiantly tried to pull out the nails which held him to the cross. Many traditional verses point to it being bad luck to kill a Robin:

"Kill a robin or a wren
Never prosper, boy or man"

Why is the Robin so popular? Perhaps because of its tameness. Robins will take worms at the feet of a gardener as he turns the soil, and will even enter our homes to take crumbs. In a sense, the tameness of the British Robin is a national compliment, for Robins in other countries are more usually shy and skulking birds, like their close relative the Nightingale. Perhaps the long tradition of not harming Robins in this country has brought about their tameness. In other countries, where they have been hunted both for the cage-bird trade and for food, Robins have quickly learned to fear man.

Outside the breeding season it is unusual to see two Robins together, an observation noted at least as early as the third century BC! "Unicum arbustum haud alit duos erithacos" (Zenodotus). This loosely translated means "One bush does not shelter two Robins". Robins are extremely territorial almost throughout the year, and in autumn males and females hold separately defended territories. If the Robin's song is in reality a war cry to defend its territory, then its red breast must be considered war paint. Actual fighting is usually avoided by the fluffing out of red breast feathers in display and, at least in the case of Robins, victory usually goes not to the strong, but to the righteous, as the owners of territories are almost always successful in defending their patch from marauding neighbours. Without a territory a Robin cannot acquire a mate or breed, hence the considerable energy with which Robins establish and defend their home areas.

The Robin's family life is strange. It is the hens which go out and choose a mate – the cocks awaiting them in their territories. For the next few months, while sharing a territory, the sexes all but ignore one another. Nest-building usually begins in March. Nests can sometimes be built remarkably quickly, as shown by the story of a gardener who hung his coat in the tool shed at 9.15am and when returning for lunch at 1.00pm found an almost completed Robin's nest in one of the pockets! Robins often nest in the strangest places – sheds, boots, old buckets or kettles and car bonnets to mention but a few!

When young Robins leave the nest they have speckled brown breasts, perhaps so that they are not mistaken for territorial rivals. Sadly the majority of these young Robins may die in their first winter. In our modern world the answer to "Who killed cock Robin?" is as likely to be a passing car or the neighbour's cat, as their more traditional enemies the stoat, weasel or Sparrowhawk. Prolonged cold weather is also fatal for the largely insect-eating Robin, and it is in late winter that bird-tables can provide a life-line for the hungry Robin.

JAY

Jays are elusive birds at the best of times and more often heard than seen. Their well known screech of alarm as you walk through woodland is often the only evidence this bird gives of its presence. A glimpse of the shining white rump as the Jay flies away, is unfortunately, our commonest view of one of the most striking of European birds.

Jays are handsome and distinctive members of the crow family, and at close range look positively exotic. The pinkish-fawn body is graced by black wings with a beautiful panel of feathers banded black and blue just below the shoulder of the wing.

September and October are two of the best months for Jay watching, as the birds are busy harvesting acorns for their winter stores. The Jay has a specially adapted oesophagus which can hold up to nine acorns. Jays search methodically under oaks for fallen acorns and then fly with oesophagus fully laden and an extra acorn held in their bills to their home grounds where each acorn is meticulously hidden. Incredibly every acorn is hidden singly, the Jay pushing its bill deep into the earth, disgorging the acorn into the cavity, and then carefully covering the hole with moss or loose earth. Several hundred, maybe even thousands, of acorns will be hidden each autumn, so a prodigious feat of memory is required to retrieve these over the winter months. It certainly seems that even when the ground is snow covered Jays know precisely where to dig, and these food caches provide their main source of food over the winter months.

Jays are almost universally hated by gamekeepers because of their probably deserved reputation as egg thieves. However, this "misbehaviour" should be balanced against the good they do as woodland guardians. The oak is almost certainly more dependent for its survival on the Jay, than the Jay on the oak! How otherwise would oak trees spread their acorns uphill! Not every acorn so carefully "planted" by the Jay will later be eaten. Some Jays will die before harvesting their winter stores, and even a Jay's memory can't be perfect. Thus over thousands of years a symbiotic relationship between oak as food provider, and Jay as tree planter has evolved to the benefit of both parties.

In the distant past, when England was a land of oak forests, Jays were presumably one of the commonest and most widespread birds. In the modern world, persecuted because of their egg thieving, and with their woodland habitat fragmented, Jays have adapted to life in suburban gardens and city parks. Doubtless few Jays live to reach the grand age of fourteen – the record for a ringed bird – but nonetheless this survivor of the wildwood will more than likely be watching you next time you go to the woods, and its derisive scream may be all that reveals the Jay, "Guardian of the Forest".

WREN

Tiny, inconspicuous and skulking the Wren may be, but despite its small size and well camouflaged appearance it is one of our most familiar birds. The Wren has featured on a British coin, the "Jenny Wren" farthing, is a favourite bird of children's stories, and is the subject of myths which probably date back to the Bronze Age. Almost everybody can recognise a Wren with its closely barred brown plumage, the short cocked tail and rather mouse-like habit of creeping around in dense cover close to the ground. It's often said to be the smallest British bird, but just loses out to the Goldcrest, which is about half a centimetre smaller!

The Wren is one of very few European species to have its origins in North America. Wrens probably spread to Europe and Asia many thousands of years ago, when there was a land bridge across the Bering Strait connecting the Old and New worlds. In Europe and Asia there is only one member of the family Troglodytidae (the cave dweller), whereas in America our Wren is known as the Winter Wren to distinguish it from some 10 other species which occur in the New world.

The Wren for thousands of years, has been a sacred bird in Europe, being the Celtic "magus avium" – magician of birds – and the Druidic bird of prophecy. In many parts of Europe there was a Wren cult during the Bronze Age. The Wren was considered sacred for most of the year, but one day in the middle of winter the Wren Hunt took place. The killing of the Wren represented the death of the dark earth powers, and the beginning of a new season of light and life. There is also the well known fable of how the Wren became King of the Birds. The birds decided that whichever species could fly the highest would become their King. When the Eagle had exhausted itself flying higher than any other bird, the Wren crept out of the feathers on the Eagle's back and flew a few feet higher!

The name Wren is of Norse origin, and means "little tail", but there are many local names including, in Norfolk and Suffolk, Bobby Wren, Tom Tit and Tiddy Wren.

For such a tiny bird, the Wren has a spectacularly loud song, said on occasion to be audible for up to half a mile. Perhaps this, together with the fact that a Wren may be heard singing virtually all year, explains why the Wren is so well known. The other explanation must surely be its adaptability. It is probably the most widely distributed bird in Britain, and thrives in a tremendous range of habitats. In Norfolk you can find Wrens on coastal marshes singing from Suaeda (sea-blite) bushes, among the marram grasses of sand dunes, on heathland, in both deciduous and coniferous woodland, and in hedgerows and back gardens, to name only some of its haunts. Really any type of land providing low cover for it to hide in, and a supply of insect food, will suit the Wren fine. Feeding entirely on insects its numbers can be devastated by a prolonged cold winter with heavy snowfall, when food becomes difficult or impossible to find. During bad weather Wrens will roost together at night to keep warm, and the record for Wrens roosting in a nest-box stands at over 50. Wrens have even occasionally been observed building mid-winter nests specifically for use as communal roosts.

In spring it is the male who builds not one, but up to six beautiful domed nests, usually constructed from moss, dead leaves and grass. The female then selects, and lines, one nest in which the 5 to 10 eggs are laid. As two broods are often raised in one season, numbers decimated after a hard winter can quickly recover given a good breeding season. This adaptable little bird remains common throughout Norfolk, which is excellent news for those who, like myself, accept this unassuming "King of Birds" as a symbol of good luck.

"... that single wren
Which one day sang so sweetly in the nave
Of that old church

...So sweetly mid the gloom the invisible bird
Sang to herself, that there I could have made
My dwelling place, and lived forever there
To hear such music".

William Wordsworth (1770 – 1850), The Prelude

JARVIS '92

KESTREL

A dark hovering silhouette above the roadside, glimpsed fleetingly as we speed past in our cars, is for most of us our usual view of Norfolk's most common bird of prey. Rather a sad reflection on our modern pace of life as this bird will reward anyone who takes a few moments to really observe its lifestyle.

Undoubtedly the Kestrel's most characteristic behaviour is its hovering – other birds of prey also hover, but the Kestrel is the master. Head motionless into the wind, tail spread and wings quivering, like a kite with no string hanging above the ground. The old English names for the Kestrel all relate to its behaviour – windhover, windfanner, windsucker or windfucker, which literally means 'to press against the wind'.

The Kestrel is easily recognised, its long pointed wings differentiating it from the similarly-sized Sparrowhawk. The male is more brightly coloured than the female with a smart reddish-chestnut back spotted black, a distinctive blue-grey head with dark moustachial stripe and a blue-grey tail with a broad black terminal tip. The female is generally duller brown and lacks the blue-grey head and tail.

Hovering is just one of several hunting techniques utilised by the Kestrel as it hunts for mice, voles or even birds and insects. Perhaps hovering is best described as 'aerial perching' and at a height of 9-12 metres gives the bird superb vantage, with its falcon eyes, of any movement in the grass below. A hovering Kestrel actually quarters the ground very methodically moving from one aerial perch to the next in its search for short-tailed voles, its favourite prey.

In winter, or during bad weather, hunting from a perch, perhaps a favourite tree, pylon or telegraph pole is actually a more common method of hunting than hovering. In severe weather, hunting from a perch uses less energy than hovering, which can make the difference between starvation and survival. A Kestrel needs a fifth of its body weight each day to survive. That may sound a lot but is roughly equal to two voles or one Starling! Kestrels will even scavenge for insects or earthworms by hopping over the ground, and in urban areas will flight-hunt, almost Sparrowhawk style, after Sparrows and Starlings.

Today the Kestrel is widespread throughout England, favouring open countryside and farmland. Like many birds of prey the Kestrel was severely affected in East Anglia by the agricultural chemicals, aldrin, dieldrin and heptachlor, used for treating seed corn. The mice and voles fed on treated seed and at the top of the food chain the Kestrel accumulated dangerous levels of these pesticides in vital organs such as the liver. During the 1950s and early 60s many birds died, poisoned by these chemicals, or were rendered infertile. The low point for Kestrel populations was reached in 1963, but with the passing of legislation limiting the use of these poisons, Kestrels made a good recovery during the 1970s and 80s.

Kestrels have proved highly adaptable, taking advantage of new habitats in urban areas, and in recently planted conifer woods. In cities, buildings form surrogate cliff nesting sites and playing fields and waste-land and building sites are favoured hunting grounds. On balance, man has probably helped the Kestrel. Church towers and old buildings provide nesting sites and the conversion of a wooded landscape to the open fields of modern farmland has undoubtedly favoured this species.

Most Kestrels probably survive less than three years. Indeed 60 to 65 per cent die in their first year of life. Causes of death range from accidents with traffic as they hunt along our roadsides, to collisions with overhead wires. Severe winter weather with continuous rain or snow also kills many birds, especially those inexperienced first year birds who are still perfecting their hunting techniques. Though the Kestrel is undoubtedly the farmer's friend, taking shrews, mice, voles and even rats, in some country areas it still falls victim to the gun, poisoning and trapping. A hovering bird makes a 'good target' for gun practice and many gamekeepers are not fond of the Kestrel.

Even nature reserve wardens do not always smile at individual Kestrels if their favoured prey is Avocet chicks, Little Terns or Bearded Tits! Individual Kestrels have done considerable damage to particular coastal tern colonies in Norfolk and Suffolk, but this is very much an exception, reflecting how the adaptable Kestrel will exploit any available food source, even Avocet chicks on the famous Suffolk Havergate Island reserve.

For most of us, the Kestrel is a welcome sight, a real bird of prey survivor, adaptable to our modern world, equally at home hunting on wild, windswept saltmarshes, or dodging pantechnicons alongside the motorway.

I caught this morning morning's minion,
kingdom of daylight's dauphin, dapple-dawn-drawn
falcon, in his riding
Of the rolling level underneath him steady air and striding
High there, how he rung upon the rein of a
wimpling wing
In his ecstasy! then off, off forth on swing. . .

Gerard Manley Hopkins (1844 – 1889), The Windhover

JARVIS (JULY)

NIGHTJAR

The Nightjar is a bird of mystery; a cryptic coloured log that explodes into life underfoot, or a disembodied voice that haunts wild heathland on warm, windless nights in May and June. The song, from which the bird takes its name, is a sustained, vibrant "churring" or "jarring" sometimes likened to the distant throbbing of a motor-bike! This sound swells and falls and is almost impossible to locate. Some individual birds have been recorded throbbing for as long as nine minutes without a pause, which is quite a feat when you consider the song contains up to 1,900 notes per minute!

During the day the Nightjar relies on its superb camouflage. Its beautiful, mottled grey-brown plumage enables it to resemble a piece of dead wood, the only give-away being the occasional movements of its large, dark eyes. When perched above the ground it characteristically lies lengthwise along a branch, its body invisible as the feather detail merges perfectly with the bark.

Like other birds of the night the Nightjar is a favoured subject of myth and folklore. A widespread and ancient story is of Nightjars stealing milk from the teats of goats, sheep and cows. The goatsucker legend goes back to at least the time of Aristotle, and its latin name (Caprimulgus) can be translated as goat milker, or goat sucker. Pliny believed that the Nightjar was blind during the day, only regaining its sight at dusk. Not only was the Nightjar reputed to take the milk of animals, it was said to poison the beasts so that they were blinded, and their udders withered away. Gilbert White, in his 18th century studies of the parish of Selborne, reported the local belief that "fern owls" did great harm to young calves by infecting them with a malady known as "puckeridge", though as a naturalist he realised that Nightjars fed entirely on insects, and their bills were far too weak to damage the hide of a cow. The only reason, of course, that Nightjars might be seen flying around and under grazing animals would be the attraction of flying insects disturbed by their grazing.

The first written Norfolk record of the Nightjar is that of Sir Thomas Browne in the 17th century, who mentions "a dorhawk conceived to have its name from feeding upon flies and beetles." The Nightjar was called a dorhawk as it feeds upon dor beetles, and its silhouette with pointed wings and tail, and fast twisting flight is reminiscent of a hawk. Other early Norfolk names include razor grinder and scissors grinder from the churring song, fern-owl from its habit of frequenting heaths with bracken, and corpse bird, an epithet given to several night birds. In the case of the Nightjar it is said that the souls of dead unbaptised children go into Nightjars and are reflected in its eerie calls!

The Nightjar is by no means a common bird in Norfolk, and the combination of its crepuscular habits, and its daytime camouflage make it a difficult species to observe. Throughout England Nightjars have declined this century, probably as a result of the rapid loss of suitable heathland habitat, which has disappeared under housing, agriculture and golf courses. There are fewer than 2,000 pairs in Britain, with Norfolk supporting some 400 pairs, about 20 per cent of the total. Their stronghold in Norfolk is now the Breckland area where cleared and recently replanted areas in the conifer forest provide good habitat. Other traditional sites include the wooded heaths of Dersingham, Sandringham, Salthouse, Kelling and Winterton.

The season for watching Nightjars is short. Some individuals don't arrive on migration until mid or late May, and many depart back to Africa by late August or early September. The breeding success is badly affected by late frosts and prolonged spells of cold, wet weather when moths and flying insects become scarce. There is some evidence that birds can become torpid in poor weather and a number of individuals have been found cold and stiff with their pulses, breathing rates and body temperatures lowered. Nightjars also have the strange habit of liking to sit in the middle of roads, only flying up at the last minute, and frequently being killed. If you do come close, their eyes glow a strange deep orange-red when caught in car headlamps!

The future of Nightjars in Norfolk, at least in Breckland, seems fairly secure. The Forestry Commission, in conjunction with the RSPB, carefully manage areas where Nightjars breed and the success of this policy has resulted recently in a significant increase in the number of pairs. Outside Breckland, the future for Norfolk's Nightjars will depend on protecting the last remnants of heathland, not only from devlopments such as new roads and buildings, but also from the natural processes whereby ancient heath becomes birch and pine woodland, and ceases to provide the open area required by the most mysterious Fern-owl.

"Lone on the fir branch his rattle notes unvaried
Brooding o'er the gloom spins the brown eve-jar"
GEORGE MEREDITH (1828 – 1909)

JARVIS 93

GREAT SPOTTED WOODPECKER

The Great Spotted Woodpecker is the true timber specialist amongst birds. This bird makes its home almost anywhere where there are trees. It is as much at home among the conifers of Thetford Forest as amongst the more refined old parkland trees of our Norfolk stately homes. Sandringham, Blickling, and Holkham are well known to this bird, but don't despair if your garden isn't on so grand a scale, because increasingly Great Spotted Woodpeckers are visiting even small town gardens, attracted to bird-tables for an easy supply of peanuts or hanging fat.

If you are lucky enough to have a "Great Spot" visit your bird-table, then you will realise what a striking and beautiful bird it is. Its smart black and white plumage with bright crimson patch under the tail, together with the characteristic alert, upright woodpecker posture, give it the air of a visiting celebrity. Other common visitors to your bird-table seem to show a certain respect when a woodpecker visits, perhaps in deference to that powerful woodpecker bill!

Some of the features which adapt this bird so well to life amongst the trees were recognised by one of Norfolk's earliest naturalists, Sir Thomas Browne. Writing in the mid 17th century he described this bird as "... remarkable in the hardness of the bill and skull and the long nerves which tend unto the tongue, whereby it stretcheth out the tongue above an inch and so licks up insecks." In fact the tongue is so long that at rest it won't fit inside the bill. Instead a thickened tube runs out of the lower jaw and up the back of the head to the top of the skull, and when not in action the tongue is retracted into this tube. The tongue, actually 5 cms long, is barbed at the tip like a harpoon, and sticky with mucus along its sides. Flicked at speed down the narrowest crevices it is a devastating weapon.

During early spring you are perhaps more likely to hear a "Great Spot" than to see one. There is no other British bird which can beat its head so hard against a tree, and do it 18 times a second! – the woodpecker's equivalent of song, which we call drumming. The woodpecker is quite selective about where it drums, deliberately choosing hollow branches which amplify the sound, and even on occasion a corrugated tin roof.

Why don't woodpeckers simply knock themselves unconscious? In fact several unique features have evolved which enable them to drum. There is no cavity between the brain and skull, so the brain remains stable and a pad of cartilage between the bill and skull acts as an efficient shock absorber. The list of special adaptations to this bird's woodpecking lifestyle is almost endless and includes the specially strengthened tail which acts as a "third leg prop" as it jauntily hops up tree trunks.

MAGPIE

Thief! Murderer! Devil! The Magpie is in serious need of a good P.R. agent. Tradition has always held that to see a Magpie is bad luck. In the past, to protect yourself against the sorrow of seeing one, it was wise to cross yourself, raise your hat to the bird, and spit three times over your right shoulder saying, "Devil, devil I defy thee!"

The name Magpie is recorded from 1605 and before that the bird was often simply known as "pie", from pied denoting a mixture of colours.

In Norfolk a local name is chatterpie, from its chattering voice, or less flatteringly maggot pie, probably derived from the 18th century word mag which denoted someone who chattered a lot.

Like other members of the crow family, Magpies will hoard food by burying it, and today anyone who hoards things may be called a Magpie. Rossini, of course, named one of his best known musical pieces, "The Thieving Magpie", and it is quite true that Magpies have a fascination with bright, shiny objects and occasionally rings and other jewellery left on a window-ledge will be seized and hidden.

Magpies are distinctive birds and provoke strong reactions, both from the gamekeeper who wishes to protect his gamebird eggs, and the songbird lover who sees the Magpie eating eggs and young of more "respectable" garden birds, such as Song Thrush, Robin or Chaffinch. In defence of the Magpie it must be said that the bulk of its food is invertebrates, especially defoliating insects and larvae.

Magpies have also recently learnt to break into milk cartons and bottles, and in doing so can spread an irritating organism called campylobacter, which causes tummy upsets.

Probably people will always love to hate the Magpie, but the next time you see one, look carefully at this "black and white" bird. Its beauty is seldom appreciated, but as it hops jauntily along, see its wings catch the light and turn to iridescent greens and blues, while the long graduated tail is a shining green, banded with purple and reddish hues.

One for sorrow, two for mirth
Three for a wedding, four for a birth
Five for rich, six for poor
Seven for a bitch, eight for a whore
Nine for a burying, ten for a dance
Eleven for England, twelve for France
ANON

SKYLARK

Any walk along the Norfolk coast on a bright summer's morning is likely to be accompanied by the sound of the Skylark. Spotting that small, dark singing speck against a blue sky is not easy! Its song makes it one of the best known of British songbirds, and perhaps only the Cuckoo and Nightingale are more famous for their calls.

On the ground the Skylark is rather nondescript; a compact looking bird, with its basic sandy-brown plumage, streaked dark brown and black above, with paler plumage below. The bill is quite thick, an adaptation for eating seeds, and it has an indistinct pale eye-stripe. The crest is not always visible, and can be raised or lowered by the bird, giving a rather square-headed appearance when lowered. A Skylark on the ground is well camouflaged and may often not be spotted until, with a liquid "chirrup", it flutters into the air on broad wings. The outer tail feathers are white, and the hind margins of the wing also appear pale; both these fieldmarks being especially noticeable when a bird is flushed from the ground.

Skylarks are birds of open ground, especially common on sand-dunes and coastal grasslands, but also at home on moors, heaths, saltmarshes and arable fields. Today, the short grass areas of golf courses are a favoured habitat. Some of my earliest birdwatching memories are of pushing my father's golf trolley to add sixpence to my pocket money, and whilst he was putting on the green I would be shading my eyes to spot the Skylarks singing overhead. Hanging on the wind on fluttering wings, the Skylark is marking its territory in just the same way as a singing bird perched on a bush. The Skylark's songpost is the air! The song is full of liquid warbling notes and trills, and may be heard between February and July, occasionally even at night. When singing, birds slowly rise sometimes to heights of well over a hundred feet. Gamekeepers used to say that if the larks rose high in the morning, then it was sure to be a fine day!

The breeding season starts early, with pairs coming together in late winter or early spring. The first clutch of three or four eggs is laid in April in a well camouflaged nest, tucked in a tussock of vegetation or in a small depression, such as a hoof-print. The young hatch after 11 days, and leave the nest as active, but flightless chicks about eight days later. About a week after the young leave the nest, the male bird becomes solely responsible for the care of the young, and the female will begin laying a second clutch. A detailed study of Skylarks in Cumberland showed that 68 per cent of eggs hatched successfully, but only 10 per cent of young still survived one month after hatching, by which time they are fully independent. In other words, from each 100 eggs laid on average only six or seven Skylarks will reach maturity.

Whilst the Skylark has been much loved by poets, it has also been the target of hunting and shooting. In the 17th century John Bunyan wrote of lark hunting:

> *"Thou simple bird, what makes thee here to play?*
> *Look, there's the fowler, prithee come away.*
> *Dost not behold the net? Look there tis spread;*
> *Venture a little further, thou art dead.*
> *Is there not room enough in all the field*
> *For thee to play in, but thou needs must yield*
> *To the deceitful glittering of a glass*
> *Between nets placed, to bring thy death to pass."*

Unfortunately for the Skylark, the belief in sympathetic magic meant that larks' tongues were thought to improve the human voice. Even today, commercial netting of larks, both for the caged bird trade and for lark pate, still takes place in many Mediterranean countries. The usual method is to use a 'call bird' – a captive bird tethered on a leather thong, whose fluttering and calling attracts passing wild larks to alight by the sprung nets which can be catapulted over the birds. There was formerly a huge trade in larks caught in England, centred on the South Downs, with Brighton as its marketing centre. Larks were exported to Paris up to the end of the last century, and a couple of hundredweight per day was not an unusual figure during the season. At roughly twenty larks to the pound, that represents over two thousand birds!

As well as the trade in larks for the table, Skylarks were also shot for sport up to the early 19th century. The "deceitful glittering of a glass" in John Bunyan's poem refers to a lark glass, which was a device of spinning mirrors that twinkled in the sunlight as it revolved. Larks appear to be hypnotised by this, and flutter near it, making them easy targets.

Today, the Skylark is found not only in its natural range from Britain and Scandinavia in the west, to Japan and China in the east, but also in New Zealand and Hawaii, where it has been successfully established by British emigrants.

In our world beset by so many troubles, the Skylark's song remains a reminder of pure and innocent joy. Its song has been described by many poets including these lovely lines by George Meredith:

> *"He drops the silver chain of sound*
> *Of many links without a break."*

An old Norfolk saying suggests that if you want to really hear what the lark is saying, then you should lie down on your back in a field and listen, an activity I can highly recommend on warm summer evenings.

> *"The giddy lark reacheth the steepy air,*
> *By sweet degrees, making each note a stair."*
> 17TH CENTURY ANON

JARVIS '92

SWIFT

A hiss of air and a black scimitar flashes past. When Swifts are feeding low, as they often do near water on wet, thundery days, they can fly alarmingly close. Accidents or collisions are remarkably rare; a testament to their speed of reaction. Swifts appear as Ted Hughes describes "at the tip of a long scream". Marauding, bandit parties of Swifts are equally at home screaming down narrow traffic filled streets in Norwich, or chasing around the chimneys of Norfolk villages. The Swift is half bird and half legend. The more we discover about this bird the more incredible its abilities seem.

Birds are creatures of the air, but the Swift has evolved to the very limits of energy conservation, speed and manoeuverability. No bird, anywhere in the world, is more at home in the air than the Swift. Its long, narrow wings render slow flight difficult. The body is superbly streamlined and in flight the tiny legs are tucked inside the body plumage to reduce drag. Even the eyes are recessed to prevent damage from wind-borne objects.

It was Gilbert White who first recognised that Swifts can mate in the air. In 1774 he wrote "If any person would watch these birds of a fine morning as they are sailing round at great height from the ground he would see, every now and then, one drop on the back of another, and both of them sink down together for many fathoms with a loud piercing shriek. This I take to be the juncture when the business of generation is carrying on."

It is only this century that the true extent of the Swift's aerial abilities has been revealed through modern techniques such as radar. Swifts not only feed and mate in the air, they even sleep on the wing. Lie on your back at twilight on a summer's evening and watch the parties of Swifts which have been screaming around the roof tops, ascending into the evening sky, often so high that they become indistinguishable dots. Swifts see very poorly in the dark, and these birds would certainly be unable to come down until dawn. Radar has confirmed that Swifts do spend all night "sleeping" high in the night sky.

Swifts are amongst the last migrants to arrive in England, often not appearing until the early days of May, and disappearing as early as late August. Their migration is believed to take them to Southern Africa, though of some 150,000 Swifts ringed in Britain only just over 100 have ever been recovered abroad. One wonders where Swifts nested before man provided house roofs. In England no example of Swifts nesting in a natural hole has been recorded for at least two centuries, though in other parts of Europe old woodpecker holes and cliff crevices do provide nest sites.

Swifts feed entirely on flying insects swept into their open gapes by stiff bristles either side of the bill. When feeding young, sometimes a food ball containing over a thousand tiny insects is held in the throat. When cold weather makes insect life sparse then Swifts will fly hundreds of miles in search of food, and the young can lower their body temperatures and become torpid.

It is now believed that the first flight of a young Swift leaving the nest lasts not for a few hours or even days, but incredibly the young bird will fly continuously for months, perhaps even years. Swifts do not breed until they are two or three years old, and never settle on the ground, only occasionally clinging to vertical surfaces. It has been calculated that an eighteen year old bird recovered in the tower of Oxford Science Museum would have flown four million miles during its lifetime – equivalent to flying to the moon and back eight times!

Next time the piercing shriek of Swifts rings in your ears, and a sickle shaped black silhouette flashes past your eyes remember that the "Devil Bird", as Swifts were once known, is alive and well, and nesting in suburbia!

To mark the swift in rapid giddy ring
Dash round the steeple, unsubdued of wing.
GILBERT WHITE (1720 – 1793)

NIGHTINGALE

The Nightingale is not an easy bird to see because of its skulking habits and fondness for dense cover. Patient watching will reveal a rather undistinguished small, brown bird, somewhat reminiscent of a large Robin in shape. Despite its unremarkable appearance this bird has undoubtedly inspired more poetry than any other British bird.

Tennyson, Keats, Shelley, John Clare and Coleridge were all amongst its admirers. Of course, it is the Nightingale's remarkable song, rather than the bird itself, which has been responsible for the almost mythic status the Nightingale has acquired. Izaak Walton, writing in 1653, describes the song beautifully:

"But the Nightingale breathes such sweet, loud music out of her little instrumental throat, that it might make mankind to think miracles are not ceased. He that at midnight, when the very labourer sleeps securely, should hear the clear airs, the sweet descants, the natural rising and falling, the doubling and redoubling of her voice might say... Lord, what music hast thou provided for the saints in heaven, when thou affordest bad men such music on earth!"

The poetic Nightingale is always female and often sad, whereas in reality the singing bird is male, and whether you regard his song as a war chant or a love song probably depends on whether you are a female Nightingale or another male.

In folklore the Nightingale is said to sing with her heart against a thorn. The story goes that the Nightingale borrowed her eyes from a serpent or slow worm, and then refused to return them. She therefore has to stay awake all night on constant guard against the snake who will take them back. Hence the thorn, and her night-time singing.

The name Nightingale means simply night singer, from the Old English "galen" to sing. Poets often named the Nightingale "Philomel" alluding to the Greek myth in which the abused Philomela, daughter of Athenian King Pandion, was changed into a Nightingale.

The best time to hear a Nightingale sing is on a warm summer evening. Nightingales do also sing during the daytime, but when other birds fall silent at dusk their true repertoire can be best appreciated when they perform as soloists. Individual birds vary in their songs; some virtuoso Nightingales are worth travelling miles to hear, whilst others are really quite indifferent singers. The question of why Nightingales sing at night has never been fully answered.

Other birds, including Grasshopper Warblers, Sedge Warblers and Reed Warblers, all of which inhabit dense cover and are furtive in behaviour, also sing quite a lot during the night. One theory put forward is that the Nightingale males, which arrive some days before the females on their spring migration, are singing to lure down females passing overhead on night migration. Whilst it is true that Nightingales are night migrants, this doesn't really explain why they continue to sing at night after they are paired. The urge to sing seems all-consuming, and during the First World War troops serving in France described in their letters home how the Nightingales continued to sing whilst shells exploded all around.

Nightingales have never been common in Norfolk, though Stevenson, in "Birds of Norfolk", observes how in the 1860s "the immediate vicinity of Norwich is particularly rich in their favourite haunts" and mentions Bracondale, Unthank Road, Earlham, Thorpe and Spixworth as particularly good sites.

Nightingales arrive in Norfolk on migration in April and May and leave in August or September. Their migration takes them across the Mediterranean and over the Sahara to West Africa and as few are ever seen in North Africa it is likely that the journey of over 1500 miles is achieved in a single non-stop flight.

In England their breeding distribution mirrors that of the cowslip and hop, occurring south of a line from the Wash to the Severn Estuary. In 1980 the British Trust for Ornithology estimated the population in England to be 4,000 – 5,000 singing males with upward of 40 per cent of the population breeding in Kent and Sussex. Sadly, the species has declined since the 1950s and perhaps our passion for tidying up rough corners of farmland, where overgrown hedges and scrubby patches of blackthorn provided favoured haunts, has contributed to this. Other factors must also be at work, however, as many areas of woodland and heath which previously supported Nightingales are deserted, though the habitat remains unchanged.

Let us hope the fortunes of the Nightingale improve so that in future many more of us will thrill to the voice of our midnight songster.

Thou light-winged Dryad of the trees,
In some melodious plot
Of beechen green, and shadows numberless
Singest of summer in full-throated ease. . .

Thou was not born for death, immortal bird!
No hungry generations tread thee down;
The voice I hear this passing night was heard
In ancient days by emperor and clown. . .

JOHN KEATS (1795 – 1821), Ode to a Nightingale

JARVIS '93

STARLING

As the winter sun westers, and the best light show in the world unfolds – sunset over Norfolk fields – Starlings fly to roost.In the distance their huge numbers look like moving clouds of smoke, and as they come closer vast swirling masses of individual birds can be seen wheeling and twisting. These evening flights can be extraordinarily dramatic and beautiful; well worth pausing to watch.

Immediately before roosting, Starlings may crowd into fields, carpeting the ground black, furiously probing the soil as they walk forward hoping for a last feed before nightfall. Individuals may move as far as 30 miles to a favourite roost site, though shorter distances of 10 to 12 miles are more usual. Favoured roost sites include reed-beds, young conifer plantations, rhododendron bushes and even buildings in city centres.

Obviously, if birds are prepared to travel considerable distances to roost together the individuals must gain some advantage from this behaviour. One benefit of communal roosting is simply crowding together for warmth. Roost sites such as reed-beds also offer protection from predators, and it has been suggested that individuals may gain information on the location of suitable feeding areas during these night-time gatherings.

You may not think of Starlings as being particularly angelic, but when radar was first invented the operators were amazed to see concentric rings appearing on their screens just after dawn to which the name "ring angels" was given. The explanation turned out to be Starlings leaving their roosts and radiating in all directions in sudden waves of hundreds of thousands of birds. A large roost could produce as many as 20 of these "ring angels".

The group name for Starlings is "murmuration", and anyone who has sat next to a winter roost will have heard the characteristic rising and falling waves of sound. Individually Starlings produce a jumble of squeaks and whistles, but they are great mimics and if you listen closely you may be surprised by Curlew whistles, Lapwing alarm calls or even the odd bar from whatever pop song is high in the charts.

Today the Starling is one of Europe's commonest birds, but as recently as the beginning of this century it was rare in Wales, Scotland, and Northern England. There are an estimated seven million birds resident in Britain, but this number increases to over 40 million in winter. In early winter walk along the Norfolk coast, on a clear crisp morning, and you will probably spot small flocks of Starlings arriving off the North Sea. British Starlings are largely sedentary, but these winter arrivals to Norfolk may have travelled from the Baltic States, Finland or even Russia.

The plumage of the Starling needs little description. Starlings live so close to us, both feeding and breeding around our homes, that we are all familiar with the species. In spring their glossy, iridescent plumage of greens and purples really is exceptionally beautiful, though in winter the gloss is less apparent, and birds take on a more heavily spotted appearance.

This is one bird which has undoubtedly adapted its lifestyle to exploit our own – whether probing our lawns for leather-jackets or noisily quarrelling for scraps of food on the bird table. I wonder if the person who released 100 Starlings in Central Park, New York, in 1890 would have been surprised that those 100 individuals have given rise to a population of 150 million, some third of the world population, with Starlings having spread from the east coast of America to the west, and from Alaska in the north to Mexico in the south.

And here and there, near chilly setting of sun
In an isolated tree a congregation
Of starlings chatter and chide,
Thickset as summer leaves, in garrulous quarrel:
Suddenly they hush as one –
The tree top springs –
And off, with a whirr of wings,
They fly by the score
To the holly-thicket, and there with myriads more
Dispute for the roosts; and from the unseen nation
A babel of tongues, like running water unceasing.

ROBERT BRIDGES (1844 – 1930), November

SWALLOW

One Swallow may not make a summer, but each year the Swallow's return is a welcome reminder of summer's approach. The Swallow is not only the most well known, and perhaps best loved, of all our summer migrants, but also one of our most attractive and graceful breeding birds.

The uniform blue-black upperparts have a wonderful metallic sheen; the forehead, chin and throat are chestnut red and the underparts white. Its relative, the House Martin, with which it is sometimes confused, is easily distinguished by its white rump, and of course the House Martin lacks the long tail streamers which make the Swallow such a graceful bird in flight. The old maxim that Swallows nest inside buildings, and House Martins on the outside, is invariably true.

Today, we readily accept the miracle of migration which each year brings our Swallows some 6,000 miles from South Africa to arrive in late April or early May, back to the very same nest site used the previous year. However, from the time of Aristotle in the third century BC until the end of the eighteenth century, there was speculation as to whether Swallows actually migrated, or simply hibernated in the mud beneath ponds and lakes! This was an understandable belief as in autumn large numbers of Swallows gather in reed-beds to roost before mysteriously disappearing, and often the first Swallows seen in spring will be flying low over water.

Through bird ringing studies, a great deal of information has been painstakingly gathered on the Swallows' migration. Most Swallows leave Britain in September, crossing the Channel and following a route through western France, across the Pyrenees and down the east coast of Spain. On crossing the Mediterranean, birds head over Morocco and Nigeria to Cameroon, before flying in a more south-easterly direction through Zaire into Botswana and finally reaching their winter quarters in the Republic of South Africa. Quite a journey, and not without its dangers. Sometimes Swallows migrating from northern Europe on a more easterly route have been caught in heavy snowfalls and prolonged rain over the Alps, and in 1974 many thousands of Swallows were rescued and later taken by train from Switzerland to Italy or southern France. Many Swallows also die on the long haul of more than 1,000 miles across the Sahara; a journey which can take two or more days with little chance to rest or find food and water. The autumn journey takes two or more months, but in spring there is much greater urgency to reach breeding grounds and the journey may be completed in a month or less. A Swallow ringed near Pretoria was discovered at a nest site in the Soviet Union 7,500 miles away, only 34 days later.

Swallows are closely associated with man, and almost without exception nest inside buildings. Old barns, or best of all a stable or cow-shed, are favoured quarters, the nest being placed on a ledge or beam, usually near the roof.

Our modern obsession with tidiness is many a Swallow's undoing. To return after a 6,000 mile journey across desert and mountains, only to find that the broken window which allowed you entry to a favoured shed has been repaired, must be somewhat galling. More serious though, for the Swallow's survival, is the change in farming affecting Norfolk. The manure heaps and old-fashioned farmyards, which provided suitable shelter and plenty of flies for food, have largely vanished.

Fortunately, Swallows remain widespread in Norfolk, especially in rural areas, and an open window will provide just as good an access to nesting areas as a broken one! The nest is built by both birds with mud collected from nearby puddles and is then lined by the female with feathers. Often pieces of animal hair will be incorporated into the nest to act as reinforcement, though the strangest Swallows' nests I ever observed were built almost entirely from cement mortar being mixed on a plastic sheet outside a barn. The Swallows seemed quite happy to accept this as a hi-tech mud substitute!

A clutch of 3-6 eggs is normal, and the young birds leave the nest 18-22 days after hatching. The logistics of feeding a brood of six young Swallows are more than a little daunting. At half-grown, an individual youngster needs on average 6,000 insects a day. And of course the adults still have to feed themselves. Remarkably, most Swallows go on to raise a second brood.

As might be expected, a bird so closely associated with man has many fascinating stories connected with it. The Romans used Swallows to convey the results of chariot races. Adult Swallows were captured and taken to the circus, and then threads, matching the winners' colours, were attached to the bird's legs. On release the adult would return to its nest site where a watcher would spot the colour of the thread.

There are several legends as to how the Swallow gained its forked tail, most relating to its theft of fire from the Devil which was brought as the Swallow's gift to the people of the world, but at the cost of singeing its central tail feathers, which never regrew. There is also the curious belief in the "Swallow Stone", a magical stone said to cure blindness. The Swallow knows the whereabouts of this magical pebble, but has to be tricked into bringing it back to the nest by the blinding of its youngsters. My favourite Swallow legend is that Swallows actually spend the winter in paradise, returning each summer to bring warmth to the earth.

The Swallow for a moment seen,
Skims in haste the village green.

THOMAS WARTON (1728 – 90)

JARVIS '92

GREY PARTRIDGE

The original stronghold of the Grey or Common Partridge was the steppe of Central Europe and Asia. Today the steppe is itself a threatened habitat, with only remnants of these once vast, open grasslands remaining. Partridges, however, have adapted to the changes agriculture has brought, and now survive in the modern "steppes" of cereal fields. Nowhere is the partridge more at home than in Norfolk's farmland.

Most people in Norfolk are familiar with partridges, even if it is only through the somewhat alarming sight of a covey whirring low over a roadside hedge to avoid a speeding car! Indeed, partridges are pretty well unmistakable: dumpy, rotund birds which prefer walking to flying. On a good day, when they are undisturbed, a partridge probably spends as little as a minute of each 24 hours in flight. The only bird which the Grey Partridge could possibly be mistaken for is the introduced Red-legged or French Partridge, which is also widespread in Norfolk. The Grey Partridge is, however, a smaller bird with a yellow bill, orange face and throat, grey neck, chestnut barred flanks, and with the male sporting a prominent dark chestnut, horseshoe-shaped patch on his lower breast.

It might be thought that a bird haunting open fields would be easy to spot, but at the first indication of danger the birds crouch low against the ground. Even in bare, ploughed fields they so much resemble round clods of earth that they are very difficult to spot. Having spotted one, wait and look more carefully, and gradually a whole covey, which usually numbers from 5 to 15 birds, reveal themselves, as various "clods of earth" begin to move and the covey resumes feeding.

The breeding season for partridges begins in February when males start to defend territories against rival males, and their rasping calls can be heard especially around sunset. Courtship between the sexes takes the form of a running chase with the cock and hen taking it in turns to pursue each other. The 10-20 eggs are usually laid in April in a well-hidden nest under a hedge, in tall grass, or in growing corn. Occasionally nests containing up to 40 eggs are found, not the efforts of an over-fertile female, but the result of two females laying in the same nest. The eggs are incubated for 23-25 days, and all hatch within a few hours of each other. Like waterfowl the young gamebirds are feathered with down, and leave the nest on the day of hatching. The young chicks feed entirely on insects, unlike their almost vegetarian parents, and develop incredibly quickly being able to make their first short flights by the age of 10-12 days.

The Grey Partridge is the most popular gamebird in Britain, and indeed is a favourite quarry species in many European countries.

The aim of the gamekeeper on many estates was to ensure as high a population as possible in late summer for the shooting season in September and October. As the numbers at this season depend very much on how many young survive, this has, in the past, led to the ruthless control of birds of prey, especially Sparrowhawk and Kestrel, but also many rarer birds such as Marsh and Montagu's Harriers met their doom in the effort to provide a good shoot.

On estates, partridges are usually shot using beaters to drive the birds over a line of standing guns. The Holkham Estate records provide some fascinating details of early shoots. For example, Mr Coke killed a remarkable 80 partridges for 93 shots in eight hours on the 7th October 1797. A record was set in November 1905 when 1,671 partridges were shot at Holkham in a single day, and during that season, 1905-6, the total bag for the estate was 8,512. Partridges can also be "walked up" being shot by walking sportsmen as they fly away, a trained retriever being used to collect the corpses. In the past, kites resembling hawks were flown to encourage partridges to crouch and sit tight whilst the hunters approached on foot.

Today the wild Grey Partridge is in trouble, with populations having dramatically declined throughout England. This long-term decline began in the 1950s, and bodies such as the Game Conservancy, have carried out considerable research into its causes. While, like most changes in bird and animal populations, no single factor can be pinpointed, certainly changes in farm practice such as the increased use of pesticides and herbicides and stubble burning are highly significant.

To help the partridge, landowners can leave the bottom of hedgerows, headlands and cereal field margins unsprayed. This practice of creating conservation headlands and field margins benefits other wildlife too, and has been shown to dramatically increase the survival of young partridge. Feeding with grain from December to March, in severe weather, will help adult birds survive the period immediately prior to the breeding season.

Sadly, releasing captive bred partridge is unlikely to increase the overall breeding population, which is determined by the availability of suitable habitat for nesting, and sufficient food supplies. In the short term, releases do of course increase the numbers of birds for the autumn shoot, but cannot be justified purely as a conservation measure.

JARVIS.

PHEASANT

The Pheasant is England's most shot at gamebird! No other Norfolk bird has its fortunes so intimately bound with man. Undoubtedly, without human intervention, the wild Pheasant population in Norfolk would fall to less than a tenth of present numbers, which are maintained purely through captive breeding, winter feeding and keepering.

The Pheasant is not a native British bird. Its natural distribution is from the Caucasus eastwards to China. There are 47 different Pheasant species in the world, and this group, with its stronghold in the Himalayas, includes the superbly plumaged Peacocks and the Junglefowl, which are the ancestors of our domestic chickens.

Our Pheasant was probably introduced to Europe by the Greeks. In mythology Jason and his Argonauts are said to have brought the Pheasant back to Greece from the valley of the River Phasis in the Colchis area. Hence the Pheasant's latin name Phasianus colchicus. The Romans certainly helped widen its distribution and most likely first brought Pheasants to England, but only as cage birds for the table. There is no real evidence of wild Pheasants until after the Norman conquest, when lords and abbots imported birds for sport and the table. At the time of Henry VIII the taking of Pheasant eggs was punishable by a year's imprisonment!

Despite many further introductions it was only at the end of the eighteenth century that the Pheasant became firmly established throughout Great Britain.

A male Pheasant is a striking bird. Its long tail is aptly described in the old poacher's name for Pheasant which is "comet". Typical birds have glossy bronze feathers marked with black, metallic blue heads, and brilliant red wattles around each eye. The female is smaller, usually light brown, and with a shorter tail. The general shape and size of both sexes renders them unmistakable, even when not typically marked. Today, because of the genetic mix, brought about by the introduction of different sub-species, it is quite possible to see plumage variations from almost black to almost white. It is likely that the Old English type, with black necks, originated from the earliest introductions from Asia Minor, whereas the Ring-necks, with white neck rings, originate from later introductions from China.

Norfolk is a stronghold for Pheasants both because cereal growing farmland, interspersed with small woodlands and hedges, is ideal habitat for Pheasants, and because of the long history and importance of Pheasant rearing for shoots. It is said that more money is spent on Pheasant management, than on looking after all other wild birds, and certainly nationally many times more money is spent privately on game management than by the government on nature conservation!

The traditional method of rearing Pheasants for the shoot was to collect eggs from wild nests which were then placed under broody bantams. Today, nearly all keepered Pheasants are produced from penned laying stock, and hatched using electronic incubators! At six weeks old the poults are moved to large pens in woodlands where they are fed and, in time, allowed to disperse.

The shooting season starts in October, though few birds are shot until November, and ends on 1st February. At shoots birds are driven by beaters to fly over a line of standing guns. Each wood, or area, is known as a drive and up to 8 areas are driven in a day. Shooting was the "respectable" method of killing a Pheasant, but poachers had their own quieter techniques. Raisins laced with rum, so the birds became so inebriated they fell from the trees, or inverted paper cones with a tit-bit at the bottom and a honeyed rim so that the "hats" would stick over the birds' heads, and allow the poacher to pick them up, are just two methods which are fairly well known!

The breeding season for Pheasants starts in February with cocks establishing territories with their explosive "kok kok" crowing and wing drumming. Males attract harems of up to a dozen hen birds, but contribute nothing to nest building, incubation or the rearing of the chicks. Some females have developed the unusual breeding habit of "egg dumping", whereby their own eggs are laid in the nests of other Pheasants, or indeed even Mallard or Partridge nests. When clutches of more than 15 eggs are found this is usually the explanation.

Pheasants were never as badly affected as Partridges by the intensification of farming in Norfolk, or the increased use of pesticides, perhaps because more of their year is spent feeding in wooded areas. Today, farming trends such as set-aside, can only help increase feeding habitat, though the decrease in traditional game-keeping has meant their arch enemy, the fox, will also benefit!

See! from the brake the whirring Pheasant springs,
And mounts exulting on triumphant wings;
Short is his joy; he feels the fiery wound,
Flutters in blood, and panting beats the ground.
Ah! what avails his glossy varying dyes,
His purple crest and scarlet-circled eyes,
The vivid green his shining plumes unfold,
His painted wings, and breast that flames with gold?
ALEXANDER POPE (1688-1744), Windsor Forest

JARVIS '93

BARN OWL

It comes as no surprise that the Barn Owl has often been associated with ghosts, and is the subject of much folklore and myth. The sudden and silent appearance of the white owl as it leaves its church tower roost at sunset, or appears as a white apparition from a gravestone perch, might well frighten the timid hearted. Even Shakespeare had little good to say about this nightbird –

"The owl shreik'd at thy birth, an evil sign." (King Henry VI)

If ever a bird deserved a better reputation, but has suffered at the hands of man, the Barn Owl is the perfect candidate. More than most birds it has long associated closely with man. Favoured roost and nest sites include ruins, churches, barns and lofts of old houses, and its preferred hunting grounds are open farmlands with hedges, rather than dense woodlands or upland moors.

There can be few birds as memorable as a Barn Owl quartering a field as the sun sets on a calm, windless late summer evening. Like people, these birds dislike strong winds and rain. Stand still and with luck the owl may pass close by, seemingly oblivious to a standing human figure, intent only on its hunting. Several reliable accounts mention owls having alighted on people's heads. To the shock of both parties one would guess!

Once you have found a Barn Owl hunting territory a return at the same time of day on a later occasion will often find the bird quartering the same field. Barn Owls are creatures of habit, often following the same hunting routes, and occupying the same territories, for many years.

There is little difficulty in distinguishing the Barn Owl from other British owls. The first impression is often of an all-white bird with a curiously buoyant flight and slow wingbeats. Periodically hovering, it usually hunts 6-10 feet above the ground, ready instantly to drop onto prey below. It will quarter a field, beating up and down the edges, sometimes taking a short rest on a convenient post to survey its territory, and when perched can turn its head through a seemingly impossible 300 degrees!

A closer look at the bird will show, however, that the plumage is not pure white. The upper parts are an attractive orange-buff, finely spotted with dark grey and white. The face is white with the curious and distinctive facial mask. Individual birds are variable with some showing orange-buff on the breast and others having pure white underparts.

The behaviour of Barn Owls has been well studied. Courtship starts in February when the birds are quite vocal, emitting blood-curdling, long drawn out hissing screams. Eggs are most often laid in late March or April, and clutch size varies with the abundance of small mammals. Most often between four and seven eggs are laid, but in a 'vole year' up to eleven is not unusual. The newly hatched young are downy and hatch at intervals of two days, allowing the older birds to kill and devour their smaller and weaker brethren if food is lacking. Such cannibalism, gruesome as it may seem with the parents sometimes tearing up a dead youngster to feed the older chick, is an adaptation to irregular food supplies, and ensures the survival of at least one or two chicks through periods of food shortage.

The owlets leave the nest at 7-8 weeks old, and are then driven from the parents' territory after about 3 weeks, usually dispersing no more than 20 miles. This behaviour is well adapted to filling any vacancies in suitable Barn Owl territories.

The Barn Owl deserves to be recognised as a true friend to man. Its diet consists mainly of rodent pests including mice, voles and rats which can be a plague to both foresters and farmers. Despite being a friend of the farmer recent changes in agriculture have done few favours for the Barn Owl. In Norfolk the change from sheep and cattle grazed grasslands, rich in voles and mice, to more intensive arable farming has seriously reduced the food supply. Driven to hunting along roadsides and railway lines the owls all too frequently fall victim to traffic. In former centuries farmers recognised the value of the Barn Owl, and provided 'owl windows' in the apex of barns to allow access for roosting and nesting. However, not everyone in Norfolk was pleased to have nesting owls and the Churchwarden's accounts for Redenhall in 1711 record 'For worke and stuff and nails in stopping out ye owles at ye church...3s 6d.' The recent boom in restoring derelict barns and farm cottages as holiday homes has doubtless deprived many Norfolk Barn Owls of their nest sites. Illegal gamekeeping, with the setting up of pole traps and poison baits on some of the more conservative estates where old traditions die hard and all birds of prey are regarded with suspicion, still pointlessly slaughters some Barn Owls each year. More serious, though, is the impact of the increasing amounts of pesticides used in modern farming. Rat poisons can kill both rat and Barn Owl.

Today the Barn Owl needs all its wits to prosper in our modern world. We are lucky in Norfolk today still to be able to enjoy the ghostly beauty of the white owl, but will our children also be able to enjoy this sight?

A greedy grave
That still for carrion carcases doth crave
On top whereof ay dwelt the ghostly owle,
Shrieking his baleful note which ever drove
Far from that haunt all other cheerful fowle;
And all about it wandering ghosts did wayle and howle.

EDMUND SPENSER (1552 – 1599), The Faerie Queen

JARVIS 93

Acknowledgements

The author would like to thank Bill Makins, Director of Pensthorpe Waterfowl Trust, for his help in obtaining out-of-print references, Sally Reynolds for typing the original manuscripts, and Michael Seago for his help and advice on specific birds.

Mrs Bertram of Bertram's Books provided valuable advice in the initial stages of publication and Susan Apling generously assisted in the design of the front cover. Thanks to Alan Gepp and Julien Lesage of Broadgate Printers for friendly advice, and design and printing skills, and to Tasha my wife, for putting up with me during the process of putting the book together.

A debt is owed to the Norfolk Journal who originally had the confidence to publish my work, and gave their support to this project. I would also like to personally express my admiration for the watercolours and line drawings by Frank Jarvis, which capture so perfectly the special character of each bird I have chosen to describe. Finally, a very large thank you to George Russell for his support of this publication.

Bibliography

"Sir Thomas Browne's Norfolk"
Extracts from the writings of Sir Thomas Browne relating to the natural history and archaeology of Norfolk in the seventeenth century.
(Larks Press 1989)

Boag, David
The Kingfisher
(Shire Natural History 1986)

Greenoak, Francesca
All the Birds of the Air
The names, lore and literature of British Birds
(Book Club Associates 1979)

Kear, Janet
The Mute Swan
(Shire Natural History 1988)

Lockwood, W B
The Oxford Book of British Bird Names
(Oxford University Press 1984)

Long, John L
Introduced Birds of the World
The worldwide history, distribution and influence of birds introduced to new environments.
(David & Charles 1981)

Munsterbury, P (Editor)
The Penguin Book of Bird Poetry
(Penguin Books 1984)

Martin, Brian P
World Birds
(Guinness Books 1987)

Nethersole-Thompson, Desmond
The Oystercatcher
(Shire Natural History 1988)

Patterson, A H
Wildlife of a Norfolk Estuary
(Methuen & Co 1907)

Patterson, A H
A Norfolk Naturalist
(Methuen & Co 1930)

Reader's Digest
Field Guide to the Birds of Britain
(Reader's Digest Nature Lover's Library 1989)

Riviere, B B
A History of the Birds of Norfolk
(1930)

Robertson, P A
The Pheasant
(Shire Natural History 1988)

Seago, M J
Birds of Norfolk
(Jarrold Colour Publications 1977)

Seago, M J (Editor)
Norfolk Bird & Mammal Reports 1986 – 1991
(Norfolk & Norwich Naturalists Society in conjunction with Norfolk Ornithologists Association)

Simmons, K E L
The Great Crested Grebe
(Shire Natural History 1989)

Stevenson, Henry
Birds of Norfolk (3 vols)
(John Van Voorst 1866)

Tate, Peter
The Swallow
(Shire Natural History 1986)

Tate, Peter
The Nightjar
(Shire Natural History 1989)

Wilson, R & Lee, P
The Marshland World
(Blandford Press 1982)

White, Gilbert
Natural History of Selborne (Ed. Richard Mabey)
(Penguin 1977)

dk phase.
Burnham
Norton.
30/6/87.
greyish